Emerging Patterns of Teaching:

From Methods to Field Experiences

Timothy R. Blair
TEXAS A&M UNIVERSITY

Emerging Patterns of Teaching:

From Methods to Field Experiences

MERRILL PUBLISHING COMPANY
A Bell & Howell Information Company
Columbus   Toronto   London   Melbourne

Published by Merrill Publishing Company
A Bell & Howell Information Company
Columbus, Ohio 43216

This book was set in Palatino.

Administrative Editor: Jeff Johnston
Production Coordinator: Sally Serafim
Art Coordinator: Lorraine Woost
Cover Designer: Cathy Watterson
Text Designer: Amato Prudente

Library of Congress Catalog Card Number: 87-61902
International Standard Book Number: 0-675-20802-5
Printed in the United States of America
1 2 3 4 5 6 7 8 9—92 91 90 89 88

To the memory of my grandmother,
Helen Burns Rawlings, a 1911 graduate of the
New Britain Normal School of Connecticut
(the present-day Central Connecticut State University)
and a teacher for fifty-six years.

Contents

Preface   *xi*

A Message to Teachers-in-Training   *xv*

CHAPTER 1
Professional Teacher Development   1
    The Changing Nature of Teaching   1
    Necessity for Differentiated Instruction   2
    Range of Instructional Goals   3
    The Importance of the Teacher   4
    Synthesis of Literature on Fostering Direct Learnings   5
    Synthesis of Literature on Fostering Inquiry and
        Understandings   6
    Defining Teaching   6
    Principles of Instruction   8

CHAPTER 2
Student Affect   13
    Concern for Affect   13
    Student Self-Perceptions   14
    Student Needs and Teaching   16
    Emotional Maturity   18
    Motivating Students to Learn   20
    Interpersonal Skills   23
    Self-Monitoring FYI: "Reading" Students   24
    Self-Monitoring FYI: Cooperative Grouping   24
    Reader Interaction 1: Student Affect   25

    Self-Monitoring Critique   27
    Summary   28
    References   28

CHAPTER 3
Classroom Management and Organization   **31**
    Managing the Classroom   31
    Elements of Successful Management   33
    Planning of Activities   33
    Managing Group Instruction   35
    Monitoring Student Progress   36
    Different Contexts   39
    Personal Characteristics of Teachers   40
    Stopping Misbehavior   41
    Self-Monitoring FYI: Pacing   41
    Reader Interaction 2: Participation Guide   43
    Reader Interaction 3: Classroom Management Problems and
        Solutions   45
    Self-Monitoring Critique   46
    Summary   47
    References   48

CHAPTER 4
Differentiated Instruction   **51**
    Types of Learnings   51
    Direct Learnings   52
    Inquiry Learnings   55
    The Planning Process   58
    Teaching a Lesson   59
    Unit Plans   64
    Flexible Lesson Planning   65
    Planning for Classroom Discussion   66
    Self-Monitoring FYI: Suggestions for Planning
        Discussion   68
    Self-Monitoring FYI: Before and After: Important
        Considerations in Teaching a Lesson   68
    Self-Monitoring FYI: "Wait-Time"   69
    Reader Interaction 4: Monitoring Instructional
        Functions   70
    Reader Interaction 5: Lesson Evaluation Report   71
    Reader Interaction 6: Constructing and Monitoring
        Classroom Questions   74
    Self-Monitoring Critique   77
    Summary   78
    References   79

CHAPTER 5
Quality Time 81

Dimensions of Time   81
Academic Learning Time   82
Examining Time Allocation   83
Independent Seatwork   86
Differential Emphasis: Control of Instructional Activities and
    Learning Outcomes   87
Self-Monitoring FYI: Time-on-Task   88
Self-Monitoring FYI: Ideas for Recreational Activities   89
Reader Interaction 7: Study of Student Time-on-Task   89
Reader Interaction 8: Observation of Seatwork
    Assignment   92
Self-Monitoring Critique   93
Summary   95
References   95

CHAPTER 6
Diagnosis and Prescription 97

The Diagnostic-Prescriptive Process   97
Standardized and Criterion Referenced Tests   99
Self-Monitoring FYI: Functional Levels of
    Understanding   104
Self-Monitoring FYI: Teacher-Made Tests   104
Self-Monitoring FYI: Record-Keeping   105
Self-Monitoring FYI: Standardized Test Reporting   105
Reader Interaction 9: Teacher Interview   106
Reader Interaction 10: Diagnosis and Prescription   107
Self-Monitoring Critique   110
Summary   111
References   112

CHAPTER 7
Variety of Materials 115

Types of Materials   115
Computer Assisted Instruction (CAI)   116
Quantity-Quality Issue   119
Personalizing Your Teaching: Teacher-Made Materials   120
Considerations in Using Materials   121
Self-Monitoring FYI: Selecting and Evaluating
    Materials   123
Self-Monitoring FYI: Using a Teacher's Guide   124
Reader Interaction 11: Classroom Materials Inventory   124
Self-Monitoring Critique   125

Summary   126
References   127

CHAPTER 8
Teacher Expectations   129
Expectations for Students   129
Teacher Efficacy   131
Summary of Effective Practices   132
Reader Interaction 12: Study of Classroom
    Interaction   134
Teacher Effort Scale   137
References   143

APPENDIX A
Sample Direct Instruction Lesson Plans   145

APPENDIX B
Sample Inquiry Learning Lesson Plans   151

APPENDIX C
Additional Seating Chart Forms   157

INDEX   159

Preface

Audience

This text is intended for teacher education students completing a generic methods course, students completing their student teaching experience, and other future teachers observing and teaching in elementary and secondary classrooms. The content of the text and its practical assignments are designed to be partially self-instructional in nature and may serve as discussion topics for generic professional education classes and student teaching seminars.

Purpose

Educational research is beginning to specify which teacher characteristics make a difference and what relationships exist between teacher performance and student achievement. School systems across the country are beginning to train teachers in principles of instruction based on what is known about teaching. Accordingly, many educators are calling for the research findings on teacher effectiveness to be incorporated into teacher preparation programs.

The purpose of this book is twofold: first, to provide future teachers with the content and strategies of effective teaching methods and second, to help future teachers develop a questioning, analytic, and self-monitoring attitude toward their own teaching.

This book will describe effective teaching strategies and provide numerous practical examples that illustrate how they may be implemented in the classroom. It will also provide diagnostic methods to help monitor one's own teaching. At appropriate intervals throughout the book examples of methods to implement the recommended teaching strategies will be provided. Also, assignments to collect data on a principle of teaching will be suggested for the reader to complete. Many of the assignments require structured observation and feedback. Also, instructors and professors are encouraged to have students work cooperatively in collecting data and in analyzing teaching techniques. These assignments serve as self-monitoring devices to help teachers-in-training become more conscious of effective instructional practices. The author agrees wholeheartedly with the many teacher educators who are calling for an increased emphasis in preservice programs on students participating and interacting vis-à-vis the teaching process with their peers and with public school and university personnel. David Berliner has called for meaningful opportunities for future teachers to discuss, practice, integrate, and learn various aspects of the teaching role with other professionals in a more laboratory-based setting (*Journal of Teacher Education*, Nov.–Dec. 1985 and Research Symposium Address at ATE Annual Conference, 1987). For students to become analytical of their attitude toward teaching, they need to have experiences that sharpen their observation skills along with opportunities to discuss these findings with their peers and interested professionals. B. O. Smith, in the book *A Design for a School of Pedagogy* (Washington, D.C.: U.S. Government Printing Office, 1980), accentuates the importance of observation. Speaking to domains of training in becoming a teacher, Smith noted: "The first domain, the one that permeates all the others, is observation. The ability to observe a phenomenon objectively is one of the primary marks of a professional in any field . . . For a teacher who cannot tell what is going on will be unable to respond appropriately and effectively to the events" (p. 84).

It is the author's contention that teachers-in-training should be exposed to teaching principles based on research and on expert opinion. Furthermore, they should have opportunities to practice these teaching principles in real classroom settings. A practical time to examine and practice effective teaching strategies is during the various "field experiences" designed for teacher education candidates. This time may be during student teaching, during an internship in the schools, or in a multitude of other clinical or early field experiences. These contacts with students and in actual classroom situations, whether brief or extended, serve a variety of purposes including learning the teaching role and gaining an understanding of learning, of students, and of the nature of schools themselves.

Although field experiences generally receive good grades from teacher education graduates, skepticism exists regarding the effectiveness of such experiences, largely due to a lack of conceptual framework or research base. The common thread in field experience programs should be those teaching principles derived from both research and expert opinion. Research in teacher effectiveness has identified teaching principles that are effective for didactic or direct teaching. Teachers who employ these instructional practices produce more learning in their classes than teachers who do not employ these practices.

Direct learning is largely assessed on standardized national tests and state-mandated basic skills tests. This learning or instruction is more formal and controlled and more concerned with low cognitive-level objectives. The other broad type of instruction is heuristic or inquiry teaching, which focuses on critical and creative skills and abilities. Although higher-level processing is not assessed on basic skill tests, it is crucial for the fully functioning learner. Inquiry instruction is more concerned with learner choice and discovery. Though there is more research on direct learning techniques than on inquiry teaching in the literature, effective teachers provide a balance between the two. To view teacher effectiveness solely in terms of direct learnings is clearly in error. Each type of instruction has its own goals and its own instructional techniques. Likewise, the outcomes of each style of teaching can be different, too, depending upon the subject area taught and the characteristics of the students—that is, age, grade level, socioeconomic level, and ability level. Despite these qualifications, research, expert opinion, and experience have specified generic teaching principles.

These generic teaching principles, which are the focus of this book, set down the conditions desirable for pupil learning and growth. Each principle actually represents a group or cluster of teacher attributes. The principles certainly do not delineate solutions to all instructional problems facing teachers. The specific applications of the teaching principles will be different depending upon a host of variables. What is important, however, is that the principles reflect what "teaching" is. Users of this book will be guided into discovering specific applications depending on their situation.

It is the sincere wish of the author that readers utilize the information presented in this book to become increasingly cognizant of what they are doing or not doing, what needs to be improved, what needs to be modified or expanded or omitted, what factors impede teaching, and how students react to what the teacher is doing. Those preparing to teach should learn where to put their time and effort. They also need to be trained as reflective, self-monitoring educators, capable of further growth and development. Students need and deserve such quality teachers, and it is the aim of this book to help produce them.

Timothy R. Blair

Acknowledgments

My thanks for their constructive and insightful reviews of the manuscript to James Raths, University of Illinois; J. Pat Knight, Appalachian State University; Henry C. Luccock, former curriculum director, Hartford Public Schools, Hartford, Connecticut; Lois Redmond, Central Michigan University; Robert Fisher, Illinois State University; and Carl Harris, Sam Houston State University, William M. Morrison, Central Connecticut State University; George Swafford, Ball State University; Jerry Thomas, Southwest Texas State University; Dennis Redburn, Ball State University; Marc Mahlios, University of Northern Iowa; and Cheryl Didham, Bowling Green State University.

Appreciation is also extended to the following school-based university student teaching supervisors for their feedback in trial versions of the in-text assignments and review of the lesson plans in the Appendix: Sandra Johnson, Becci Rollins, Linda Cress, Anna Seaman, Michelle Hart, Ernest Kelly, Margaret Moore, June Ferguson, Virginia Smith, Karen Raymond, Kathy Busby, Lynda Haynes, and Marsha McCord.

I would like to thank Norma Hinojosa for her patience and careful typing of the entire manuscript. I must also express my thanks to the Merrill staff, especially to Jeff Johnston for his expertise and good judgment.

Most of all, my thanks go to my wife, Jeanné, and my two sons, Tim and Billy. Without their support and critical assistance, this book would never have been completed.

A Message to Teachers-in-Training

Importance of Being a Self-Monitor

As a teacher-in-training, you are eager for reliable information on how you can be an effective teacher. The purpose of this text is to further your progress in becoming a professional teacher. Principles of instruction from the research on teacher effectiveness will be presented and discussed in each chapter. You will be encouraged to apply and reflect on each principle of instruction in your own subject(s) and classroom. After a succinct discussion of each principle of instruction, many practical suggestions will be given to help you improve your teaching. Unfortunately, no simple formula can be given for all classrooms. A formula for effective instruction for all students, regardless of age, grade, interests, needs, learning style, and learning rate is incompatible with our knowledge of students and learning. What is compatible with it, however, is the development of a self-monitoring, reflective attitude that generates useful information about the students, the subject being taught, the classroom environment, and possible teaching strategies to accomplish your goals.

This text is based on the following proposition: Teachers who engage in a process of monitoring their own teaching become more confident in their abilities and are able to provide the instruction students need. An approach to teaching based on this proposition encourages you to become a self-monitor. Self-monitors reflect about their teaching and ask, "why am I doing what I am doing?" By becoming a self-monitor, you will be able to recognize student needs and determine the right course of action. Self-monitoring should be a continuous process that makes you cognizant of strengths and weaknesses in an instructional program and points the way for further diagnosis or modification of the existing program. The process of self-monitoring is facilitated by systematically observing classroom events and by having a friend or colleague observe and provide feedback on your teaching. Once you have collected information on your teaching, you are in a position to reflect on the information and discuss your perceptions with your college supervisors, cooperating teachers, and fellow teachers-in-training. Through this process of reflection, you will improve the learning in your classroom and become more confident in your teaching abilities. This process of self-monitoring is depicted below:

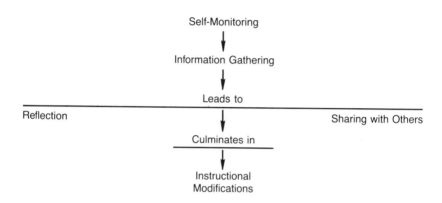

Becoming a Self-Monitor

Beginning with Chapter Two, each chapter will focus on one principle of instruction, synthesize important information regarding the principle, present methods to implement that principle of instruction in the classroom, and, most important, explain how to be a self-monitor for the principle of instruction being discussed. This is accomplished in three ways:

1. *Reader Interaction* segments offer in-text assignments.
2. *Self-Monitoring FYIs (For Your Information)* contain a full spectrum of teaching tips, ideas, and useful information.
3. *Self-Monitoring Critiques* are brief, thought-provoking questions at the end of each chapter.

The chapters will provide in-text activities and assignments to involve you and help you monitor your teaching, for instance, by interviewing a teacher or having another student teacher or your cooperating teacher observe and record data on an aspect of your instruction. These in-text self-monitoring assignments are labeled *Reader Interaction*. For example, a *Reader Interaction* assignment on the principle of providing differentiated instruction asks you to examine the type of comprehension questions you pose to students during a lesson. Part of the assignment requires you to tape one of your lessons (so you can analyze the results) or have another student teacher or your cooperating teacher tally the type of questions you ask students (according to Bloom's taxonomy). By collecting this information, reflecting on the results, noting patterns and tendencies, and perhaps sharing the results with other students in a seminar or university class, you can improve your questioning techniques and thereby improve the quality of instruction. These *Reader Interaction* assignments provide specific questions needed to gather precise information to pinpoint areas in need of attention.

A second way to help you implement a self-monitoring attitude is the inclusion of short, informational segments labeled *Self-Monitoring FYIs* in each chapter. Each FYI focuses on an important topic related to the principle of instruction being discussed. The FYIs will provide you with practical information and teaching tips, points to remember and brief discussions and explanations. You are encouraged to reflect on the information as it relates to your own situation, to try the ideas in classroom, and to discuss the information with others.

The third way you will be encouraged to be a self-monitor in relation to your teaching is to reflect on the brief listing of questions at the end of each chapter labeled *Self-Monitoring Critique*. Each critique lists concluding questions to reflect on regarding the principle of instruction covered in the chapter. You are encouraged to discuss these questions with other students and teachers.

There are numerous methods of implementing the various principles of instruction, and it is hoped you will adapt them to your own style. Furthermore, there is no one "correct" method—but many styles depending on the situation. For each principle of instruction, it is recommended you try it out in one or more classes and ask yourself: "How does it work? Why did it happen this way? How might it work better next time?" In this way, you will not only be learning the principles of instruction and fitting them to your situation but also developing ways to monitor your teaching. The ability to observe yourself honestly, monitor your teaching, and modify your teaching is a hallmark of a true professional.

CHAPTER 1

Professional Teacher Development

The Changing Nature of Teaching

The emphasis in teacher training has shifted many times since the turn of the century; however, the basis has always been the same—to train future teachers better so that they will teach our students more effectively. As you move forward in your teacher preparation program, it is crucial to continually realize your importance as a member of the teaching profession. As a teacher, you will have a profound influence on each student you teach, not only intellectually but personally and emotionally. Regardless of the background of your students, what you teach, how you teach, and how you treat students will have lasting effects on every student in the classroom. You hold the keys to helping students live a full life. Henry Adams said it best when he stated, "Teachers affect eternity; they never know where their influence will end." Only the profession of teaching can make this claim.

We have all had teachers whom we considered excellent. However, only recently has research on teaching begun to identify the qualities these excellent teachers exhibited in the classroom that made them so effective. Today's teachers need a greater and broader knowledge base, and it is evolving at a rapid pace (Corrigan, 1982). New teacher education programs are being designed and older programs revamped to better prepare the teachers of tomorrow. One major way to acquire this knowledge base is through the field experiences you are completing or will be required to complete. Therefore, the current emphasis is on beginning teaching experiences that incorporate the teaching principles gleaned from research. This is not to suggest that teachers educated twenty-five or thirty or more years ago were ill prepared to perform their jobs; however, recent research on teaching has identified common components that are linked to quality experiences for students. It is these tenets of effective teaching that you will be asked to try out in the classroom.

Necessity for Differentiated Instruction

A true story that has been repeated many times involves school board members who try their hand at substitute teaching. Invariably the teaching does not last very long. The eye-opener, in addition to the obvious concern for classroom management, is that students are different. This one fact (there are very few facts in education) is what makes teaching so intrinsically satisfying and at the same time so difficult. Students are different, and they differ in a multitude of ways—in intelligence, social awareness, emotional maturity, psychological well-being, cultural awareness, physical maturity, thinking abilities, creativity, ability levels in various subjects, and threshold of pain, to name a few. Also, in every class there is a range of student ability. For example, the typical second grade class will have students who range from first grade through fourth grade reading level, and students in a typical tenth grade class will range from fifth grade level through college level. What makes teaching so rewarding and challenging is that you must teach twenty to thirty different students in one class at the same time. In addition to meeting the individual needs of the students, you inherit the demands of meeting their needs in a whole class setting. The constraints of the classroom itself—the desks, chairs, tables, materials, a 40' by 40' room plus students—can challenge the best of teachers. Teachers must orchestrate all to provide instruction that will help students learn.

Differentiated instruction is a demanding task, especially when one fully realizes the constraints placed on teachers. Although differentiated instruction has been a teaching goal for years, the truth is it is not being practiced in many of our schools. Far too frequently, lip service is paid to meeting the varied needs of all students. In reality, many students are given the same instructional program in spite of their individual differences. When the same program for all students does not work, some students then become a "problem." There is a lack of recognition of the wide range of individual differences in a class and a lack of differentiated instruction to meet student needs. Westbury (1973) contends that the reason for a lack of differentiation is the constraints of the classroom environment itself. He feels that all teachers have four constraints or needs placed upon them while operating within a classroom:

1. To cover a certain amount of material
2. To make sure students master or learn the material
3. To control affect (attitudes and feelings)
4. To manage the class (discipline)

Each day teachers must deal with these constraints or pressures. Depending on the teaching situation, certain pressures may monopolize a teacher's attention. For example, at one time a teacher may be concentrating on student mastery of the task at hand. At the same time, this concern for mastery may conflict with coverage, affect, and management. Another example of emphasizing one concern with consequences that affect another is when a specific time limit is assigned for a topic without concern for student mastery. As a teacher you inevitably must make compromises between the four constraints, but you should work to discover the proper combination that leads to increased student learning. Finding the proper combination of course depends upon your instructional goals, since a teacher teaches differently for different goals. You are encouraged to juggle these constraints, trying various methods of teaching and evaluating their effectiveness. Many times, a concentration on a constraint is exactly what you want, even though you sacrifice an area of concern. For instance, you may loosen the reins on grouping procedures to advance student cooperation and peer tutoring; by doing so, however, you sacrifice student time-on-task and thus mastery. By utilizing Westbury's framework, you can better understand the teaching process and potential problem areas and thus differentiate instruction more effectively based on your style of teaching, your students, and the instructional program.

Range of Instructional Goals

In addition to the demands of the classroom itself and the range of student ability, as a teacher you must be concerned with the broad spectrum of instructional goals. The goals of instruction at any grade level span three areas of learning: developmental or instructional, independent or recreational, and corrective. Although each grade level and subject area will differ with respect to the three instructional goals, each grade and subject area should include experiences in each area.

The developmental or instructional phase includes the systematic learning of knowledge, skills, and content in a subject area. This phase of learning is usually given the largest amount of allocated time in today's curriculum. Teachers are expected to cover a certain amount of material and students are expected to master or learn this material. This instruction is based on a diagnosis of learner needs and is suited to individual needs whether a student is performing below grade level or is a gifted learner. Included in the developmental learning area is an application phase, in which students are provided experiences to practice the skills taught. Explaining something new to students is not enough to ensure student mastery. Teachers must provide interesting and varied practice on new learnings if students are to learn new content.

In the independent or recreational phase, students apply their new skills and content to expand their interest and knowledge in a particular subject. They usually accomplish this through classroom, library, and home research projects or recreational reading. New knowledge is easily lost if students cannot or do not use it in their outside reading or in new learning situations. Though you may suspect that a mastery of basic knowledge in a subject area automatically leads to increased independent learning, a study by Blair and Turner (1984) indicated that this may not be the case. As part of a status study of reading attitudes and interests, the perceptions of middle school students were assessed regarding how well basic instructional materials fostered independent learning habits. Surprisingly, almost

50 percent of the students felt their basic instructional materials did not help them learn in other school subjects or help in the development of independent learning habits. Students need to make specific efforts to bridge the gap between mastering basic content and using that knowledge to learn on their own. After all, the ultimate success of an instructional program has to be judged by the degree to which students can apply their knowledge in independent learning situations.

Last, due to the reality of individual differences, each teacher needs to be concerned with ways of correcting and reteaching important knowledge and skills. Not all students will grasp new content in the same way or at the same rate. Thus, teachers need to reteach new knowledge in a variety of ways. The corrective program takes place in the regular classroom and is part of the ongoing program.

The Importance of the Teacher

The most pervasive conclusion of teacher effectiveness studies from the early 1970s is that you, the teacher, have a profound influence on how much students learn (Berliner, 1979). Not long ago, information on specific characteristics of successful teachers was difficult to find in the literature. In an exhaustive study sponsored by the President's Commission on School Finance, the Rand Corporation assessed the current state of knowledge regarding the determinants of educational effectiveness (Averch et al., 1971). Perhaps the commission's most revealing conclusion was that research has yet to find anything that consistently and unambiguously makes a difference in student achievement. The report indicated that there was considerable evidence that non-school factors may be more important in determining educational outcomes than are school factors. The relationship between non-school factors and student achievement is significant. However, this relationship is less significant when one looks at gains in student achievement rather than general levels of achievement.

Since that time, further studies have demonstrated that educational researchers overlooked factors relating to teacher effectiveness. Rather than amassing data at the school level, more recent investigations have looked at what goes on inside classrooms. In so doing, researchers identified several practices and factors that explain why students in some classrooms seem to learn more than students of similar ability learn in other classrooms (Brophy & Good, 1986; Hutchins, 1987).

Rather than focusing on a student's background or socioeconomic level, researchers have identified teacher practices that when applied appropriately with students in a particular subject and grade level lead to successful learning. These teaching practices are positive and optimistic in nature because teachers have direct control over implementation in the classroom. It is crucial to differentiate between those factors over which you have direct control in the teaching-learning process and those over which you do not have direct control. You have little control over a student's socioeconomic level, a student's previous school problems, overall school climate, and administrative leadership in your school. However, you have direct control over many of your face-to-face interactions with students and the manner in which you utilize instructional time. In these situations you as a teacher can positively influence students.

Motivated by the emphasis on literacy, accountability, and standardized testing, the majority of research on effective instruction has been in the area of direct learning and skills (Rosenshine, 1979), which needs to be differentiated from learning that fosters inquiry, critical understandings, appreciations, and problem-solving abilities. In the area of direct learning and skills, the teacher is the central figure and direct instruction is emphasized (i.e., teachers select and direct class activities). In fostering inquiry, the teacher first explains the process, followed by student exploration and discovery. Both types of learning—direct and inquiry—are the responsibilities of teachers. Differences in teaching strategies for direct and inquiry learnings will be discussed in future chapters.

Typically, effectiveness has been defined in terms of increased student achievement in the learning of formal knowledge, facts, skills, procedures, and so forth. However, in contrast to this narrow focus of teacher effectiveness, which emphasizes only direct learning, effective teachers have always considered student growth in inquiry and discovery processes to be basic to being a literate person and have included instruction on the learning of higher cognitive level objectives. Indeed, the effective teacher provides opportunities for students to learn both necessary content and inquiry abilities. The discussion of teacher effectiveness throughout this book will reflect both types of learning. A brief summary of the teaching skills of the two is presented below.

Synthesis of Literature on Fostering Direct Learnings

Studies of teacher effectiveness have indicated that teachers who exert greater than average effort in both covering the necessary content and maintaining student attention (time-on-task) in academic activities produce greater than average learning in their classes (Rosenshine, 1979). Effectiveness has been defined as significant achievement gain on standardized tests. Thus, most research on effective teaching has focused on teaching basic knowledge and skills in various subject areas. Covering the necessary content entails providing students with the opportunity to learn whatever it is you expect them to learn. This means allocating sufficient time for a particular subject or topic. The concern for maintaining student attention or student engagement in learning is due simply to the following formula: greater student attention equals greater student learning. To ensure a high degree of student attention or engagement, teachers must be good classroom managers. Teachers need to provide structured learning and be in control of the class. This structured learning method is usually called "direct instruction" and is effective for learning an ordered body of content (Rosenshine, 1983). The content for instruction is taught in small steps with close monitoring or checking by the teacher. Student involvement is guided by the teacher using modeling procedures and step-by-step explanation. The pacing of instruction is kept at a relatively rapid rate to hold student attention. All this teacher-directed instruction is accomplished with minimal unproductive or "down" time in a positive, warm class atmosphere. Teachers hold high expectations for students and communicate this attitude to them through actions (Brookover & Lezotte, 1977). Overall, one secret to improved student learning is maintaining a high degree of interaction between the teacher and student (McDonald, 1976).

Synthesis of Literature on Fostering Inquiry and Understandings

One of the major goals of our educational system is to teach students to think for themselves. Effective learners not only can pass midterm and final examinations and functional literacy and basic skill tests but seek out information and know how to use what they have investigated. Most of the research on teaching has focused on mastery of information that can be stated in behavioral, objective form. However, effective teachers have always engaged students in activities not easily amenable to behavioral, objective statements (Raths, 1971). Indeed, the consensus in the educational literature is that teachers can enhance students' inquiry abilities through planned instruction and creative assignments (Benderson, 1984).

Research on teaching is beginning to indicate that teachers need first to make sure their students understand a particular inquiry skill and then to provide numerous activities to try out and integrate this learning (Beyer, 1985; Kierstead, 1985). Allocating sufficient time for inquiry learnings in the classroom is imperative. However, the mere allocation of time is not enough; students also need explanation, clarification, and guidance by the teacher. The initial learning of an inquiry ability is best done through explanation by the teacher. However, the application of various inquiry skills to real-life situations and independent study assignments is best achieved through a more student-centered approach. In developing inquiry skills, there is less concern for closely supervised student attention and for briskly paced instruction but more for allocating sufficient time for students to study either individually or in small groups. Most important, instruction for inquiry goals changes the role of the teacher from someone who controls, directs, and guides all learning (as in direct instruction) to a helper and facilitator.

Defining Teaching

Today, as in years past, teaching is a major challenge and a complex process. Defining teaching is not as easy as one might think, since there are many facets to the process and many philosophies and approaches to the teaching task. One can attempt to define the teaching process in a general sense by stating that teaching involves those attitudes, skills, and abilities needed to guide student learning. More specifically, teaching can be defined descriptively by describing those teaching behaviors necessary to foster both direct and inquiry learning (see Chapter Four). This method of analyzing the teaching process by describing what teachers do when they teach has been used in past years. Louis Raths (1969), for instance, formulated a list of the major teaching functions of every teacher that was the result of over twenty-five years of study and discussion with thousands of teachers.

The Ten Components of Teaching
1. Informing and explaining
2. Showing how
3. Supplementing the curriculum
4. Providing children with opportunities to think and to share their thoughts with others
5. Helping children to develop values
6. Relating school and community
7. Creating opportunities for each child to earn status and respect among his [or her] peers
8. Creating a secure emotional atmosphere to facilitate learning
9. Diagnosing and remedying learning problems
10. Recording and reporting (p. 27)

Green (1971) also analyzed what teaching is by observing what teachers do. Viewing teaching as a practical activity, he categorized the essential activities of teaching under the general headings of *logical* and *strategic* acts (p. 4).

The Logical Acts
1. Explaining
2. Concluding
3. Inferring
4. Giving reasons
5. Amassing evidence
6. Demonstrating
7. Defining
8. Comparing

The Strategic Acts
1. Motivating
2. Counseling
3. Evaluating
4. Planning
5. Encouraging
6. Disciplining
7. Questioning

According to Green, logical acts are "those activities relating primarily to the element of thinking or reasoning in the conduct of teaching" and strategic acts "have to do primarily with the teacher's plan or strategy in teaching, the way material is organized or students are directed in the course of teaching" (p. 4). There are interesting similarities between Raths's and Green's conceptions of teaching. Both of their lists were compiled for the purpose of describing what teachers do. Raths stated: "The whole document in its entirety is a way of asking:

Does this person simply work in the classroom, or is he teaching?" Green asserted: "Activities associated with the logic and strategy of teaching are indispensable to the conduct of teaching wherever and whenever it is found." Neither evaluated the quality of the components or activities; both stressed only the fundamental elements. Among the differences are that Green explicitly mentioned motivating and disciplining, while Raths's components included direct attention to developing values of students and the teacher's professional role both outside and inside the classroom in relating the school to the community. These two ways of thinking about teaching can make you increasingly aware of what teachers do in the classroom and thus help you to grow continually in your profession. You should consider each of these views in relation to the principles of instruction listed in the next section of the chapter and in the subsequent chapters that deal with each principle.

Principles of Instruction

One frequently hears that we in the educational profession do not know what makes an effective teacher. Impressions of experience and the recent emphasis on examining what goes on in classrooms of effective teachers have yielded principles of teaching that when applied appropriately enhance student learning and growth. While acknowledging that teachers have a long way to go, we must affirm that we do indeed know some characteristics of effective teachers. Teaching is a decision-making process, and the judgments teachers make are the real keys to the success or failure of their program. Teachers can expend their time and effort in a variety of ways in teaching, and research on teaching has helped us discern which efforts are more helpful than others in teaching, since clearly not all efforts in teaching are helpful. A solid foundation in teaching should begin with insights gleaned from studying teaching. You as a teacher-in-training should realize that your commitment to teaching is crucial; more important, you should be aware of the areas in which your efforts should be expended. The following principles of instruction provide a foundation by specifying seven areas of concern. Thus, the quality of life in the classroom and academic achievement can be enhanced when teachers do the following:

1. cultivate student feelings and emotions;
2. maintain effective classroom control;
3. provide an appropriate balance between fostering direct learnings and inquiry abilities;
4. maximize the use of classroom time to teach students what they need to know;
5. diagnose student strengths and weaknesses and provide instruction based on student needs;

6. use a variety of materials to teach what their students need to know;
7. and believe in their abilities as teachers to make a difference and convince their students that they will learn.

These seven principles of instruction emphasize processes of teaching, processes about which you can gather information while observing and teaching in a classroom. With the exception of chapters Two, Three, and Eight, each chapter is independent, and the book can be read in any sequence. The first chapter deals with student feelings and emotions. The rationale for discussing affect first was to highlight the basic philosophy that for students, learning and feelings are interdependent. To begin a study of teaching processes on any other note would be to ignore a fundamental human characteristic. Success in teaching would be hollow without a pervasive awareness and concern for student affect in the learning process. Experts in instructional and management techniques who fail to cultivate student attitudes and feelings reduce their skill to that of a technician, as opposed to a professional concerned with developing individuals to the full extent of their capacity. Chapter Three synthesizes important learnings in the area of classroom management. This chapter comes at an early stage in the text because of the primary importance of this topic for both student teachers and teachers in our schools. Classroom management is the major area of concern for student teachers. Before you will feel comfortable and motivated to gauge the impact of your instructional techniques and implement new teaching methods, you must feel safe and in control of the classroom environment. Stated another way, control precedes technique—managing the classroom environment successfully precedes the application of effective teaching techniques. Chapter Eight focuses on teacher expectations, the process of self-monitoring, and key understandings from each previous chapter. You will be encouraged to think back to each principle of instruction and the structured feedback given on different aspects of your teaching and assess your own strengths and weaknesses. In this way, you will be able to note any discrepancies between where you are and where you would like to be with respect to your teaching style.

The principles of instruction are presented as working hypotheses to be implemented and tested in teaching situations. They serve as a foundation for studying teaching. Most important, the principles should not be accorded the status of universal truths for all students, all content areas, and all grade levels. Just the opposite is true—you will be able to implement these principles successfully in different doses depending upon the students in your class, the content you are teaching, the grade level you are teaching, and your style and personality. Each teacher has a particular style; your job is to shape your style to be effective in your own situation. Remember, though effective teachers have different styles, they can produce the same positive results. To become a professional decision-maker you will need to have a healthy attitude toward any teaching strategy and to monitor that strategy's effect on students. Because teacher judgment is the key to effective instruction, it is important to give these principles close scrutiny, to experiment with them, and to modify them depending on your situation.

References

Averch, H. A., et al. (1971). *How effective is schooling? A critical review and synthesis of research findings.* Santa Monica, CA: Rand Corporation.

Benderson, A. (1984). *Focus: Critical thinking.* Princeton, NJ: Educational Testing Service.

Berliner, D. (1979). Tempus educare. In D. Peterson & H. Walberg (Eds.), *Research in teaching: Concepts, findings and implications.* Berkeley, CA: McCutchan.

Beyer, B. K. (1985). Teaching critical thinking: A direct approach. *Social Education, 49* (4), 297–303.

Blair, T. R., & Turner, E. (1984). Skills instruction and independent learning. *Middle School Journal, 15,* 6–7.

Brookover, W. B., & Lezotte, L. W. (1977). *Changes in school characteristics coincident with changes in student achievement.* Occasional Paper No. 17. East Lansing, MI: Michigan State University, College of Urban Development. (ERIC No. ED 181 005)

Brophy, J., & Good, T. J. (1986). Teacher behavior and student achievement. In M. C. Wittrock (Ed.), *Handbook of research on teaching,* (pp. 328–375). (3rd ed.). New York: Macmillan.

Corrigan, D. (1982). Curriculum issues in the preparation of teachers. Invited address delivered at the World Assembly of the International Council on Education for Teaching, Rome, Italy.

Green, T. F. (1971). *The activities of teaching.* New York: McGraw-Hill.

Hutchins, T. F. (Ed.). 1987. *Effective classroom instruction.* Bloomington, IN: Phi Delta Kappa Center on Evaluation, Development, Research.

Kierstead, J. (1985). Direct instruction and experiential approaches: Are they really mutually exclusive? *Educational Leadership, 42,* 25–30.

McDonald, F. I. (1976). *Beginning teacher evaluation study, Phase III, Summary.* Princeton, NJ: Educational Testing Service.

Raths, J. (1971). Teaching without specific objectives. *Educational Leadership, 28,* 714–720.

Raths, L. E. (1969). *Teaching for learning.* Columbus, OH: Merrill.

Rosenshine, B. (1979). Content, time and direct instruction. In H. Walberg & P. Peterson (Eds.), *Research in teaching: Concepts, findings, and implications.* Berkeley, CA: McCutchan.

Rosenshine, B. (1983). Teaching functions in instructional programs. *The Elementary School Journal, 83,* 335–352.

Westbury, I. (1973). Conventional classrooms, open classrooms and the technology of teaching. *Journal of Curriculum Studies, 5,* 99–121.

Principles of Instruction

- **Cultivate student feelings and emotions.**

- Maintain effective classroom control.

- Provide an appropriate balance between fostering direct learnings and inquiry abilities.

- Maximize the use of classroom time to teach students what they need to know.

- Diagnose student strengths and weaknesses and provide instruction based on student needs.

- Use a variety of materials to teach what the students need to know.

- Believe in your ability as a teacher to make a difference and convince students that they will learn.

CHAPTER 2

Student Affect

Concern for Affect

"The teacher is the single most significant factor in determining whether students will be successful in learning" has become something of a cliché among educators today. This statement implies a knowledgeable, skillful, exciting, and caring teacher. We have all had teachers like that, who enjoyed what they were doing and instilled a love for learning in their students. These teachers put life into the subjects they taught and cared deeply about their students as human beings. Such teachers were concerned with not only the cognitive growth of their students but also how their students felt about themselves and their abilities to be successful. In short, these teachers found the right mixture of cognitive and affective concerns. Rogers (1987) spoke to this very issue as he discussed questions he would ask of himself if he were a teacher:

> Can I help the student develop his feeling life as well as his cognitive life? Can I help him to become what Thomas Hanna calls a soma—body and mind, feelings and intellect? I think we are well aware of the fact that one of the tragedies of present-day education is that only cognitive learning is regarded as important. (p. 121)

That students' self-perceptions and feelings prompt cognitive outcomes, and vice versa, is well known (Beane & Lipka, 1984). Discussing directly how feelings relate to one's actions, Rubin (1973) stated:

> The point . . . is that feelings can aid or hinder the cognitive process. Properly taken into account, they can make a subject more interesting, learning more easy, motivation more personalized, and behavior more productive. It is

imperative that thought (cognition) and emotion (affect) be integrated so that one informs the other. (p. 15)

However, a total emphasis on cognitive goals with no concern for affect may produce students who may pass tests but most likely will acquire a negative attitude toward learning. Without a proper mixture of cognitive and affective concerns, life in the classroom can become boring and dull. With it, however, teachers can make the learning experience both exciting and worthwhile. Regardless of the level you are teaching or observing, it does not take long to notice the positive and negative consequences of student emotions on success in school. Being in the classroom and learning should be a pleasant and successful experience for all students. If students learn to enjoy learning, they will want to continue to learn once their formal schooling ends (Gambrell & Wilson, 1973).

Student Self-Perceptions

Since feelings are clearly linked to student learning, let us as a first step in looking at the teaching process review the importance of self-perceptions in learning. According to Beane and Lipka (1986), self-perceptions have two dimensions: self-concept, which is "the description an individual attaches to himself or herself" (p. 5), and self-esteem, which "refers to the evaluation one makes of the self-concept description and, more specifically, to the degree to which one is satisfied or dissatisfied with it, in whole or in part" (p. 6). The authors describe the two broad influences in forming self-perceptions, which are the individual self and one's environment. Factors influencing the individual self include one's values and beliefs, assumptions about one's self and other people, attitudes, and needs. Environmental factors that have a major influence on one's self-perceptions include the home, the classroom itself, the curriculum, other people (both in and out of school), and, most important, the teacher. Of course, these factors have been at play since birth and are constantly interacting. Students who feel good about themselves are not afraid to learn something new and are interested in new experiences, whereas students who have developed negative self-perceptions are less confident and do not feel worthy. Thus, these students are often not open to new experiences in school because they perceive of these experiences as another opportunity to fail. A person's approach to any activity is influenced by prior experiences and his or her accumulated perceptions of such activity. Even though changing a student's negative self-perception is not easy, it can be accomplished over time by a caring, enthusiastic teacher. Figure 2.1 presents student behaviors indicative of positive and negative self-perceptions. Although no single incidence of a behavior should be interpreted as definitely indicating a low or high self-perception, systematic observation of students will provide you with an overall view of how your students view themselves and serve as a guide to track changes in individual students' self-perceptions.

The person who is developing and maintaining clear and positive self-perceptions typically:

   is willing to take risks

   expresses opinions and ideas, even when they may be unpopular

   is eager and willing to take on new problems

   is willing to become involved in group interaction

   asks questions in search of self-understanding

   can function in an ambiguous and flexible environment

   is willing to assume leadership

   brings in materials from hobbies or interests

   draws examples from his or her experiences in expressing ideas

   is willing to assume responsibility

   shows interest in new ideas and is willing to examine them openly

   is concerned about the feelings of others

   avoids situations that have self-destructive potential

   is willing to deviate from the group if the group is seen
      as nonconstructive

   cares about personal physical health

   enjoys seeing others succeed

   follows through with tasks

   shows confidence in his or her work

   is willing to show personal work to others

   refers to self in positive terms

   accurately assesses his or her work

   is optimistic about his or her future

The person whose self-perceptions tend to be unclear or negative frequently

   is overdependent on teachers and other "authorities"

   is obsessed with conforming to others' standards

   avoids expressing personally held ideas or opinions

   rejects new ideas or alternative explanations

   criticizes others to make himself or herself look better

FIGURE 2.1 *Behaviors that may indicate the quality of self-perceptions (From* Self-Concept, Self-Esteem, and the Curriculum *[pp. 126–127] by J. A. Beane and R. P. Lipka, 1986, New York: Teacher's College. Copyright 1986 by Teachers College Press. Reprinted by permission.)*

avoids new or complicated problems

is reluctant to meet new people or interact in a group

avoids leadership roles, even when asked by the group

refuses to talk about personal interests, hobbies, and the like

rarely asks questions that search for personal meanings

has few or no interests other than those assigned by others

ignores the feelings of others

unthinkingly exposes self to destructive situations

does not take care of self physically

constantly demonstrates a need to prove self-worth

easily gives up when problems or difficulties are encountered

depends on others for answers or solutions to problems

refers to self in negative terms

over- or underestimates his or her own work

is pessimistic about his or her future

is very inconsistent, constantly changing his or her mind

cannot make decisions

FIGURE 2.1—Continued*

Student Needs and Teaching

What makes one student more successful in learning than another? Certainly self-perception plays a key role. Another powerful factor is the fulfillment of personal needs. According to this concept, a person performs according to his or her perceived needs in the classroom. Students and adults generally act in ways that make sense to themselves. The best learning occurs when a student both feels a need to know something and believes he or she has a reasonable chance of success. Since students have different needs, teachers must learn to recognize these needs and try out numerous options when interacting with students. Addressing this point, Ausubel and Robinson (1969) stated:

> Since teachers are constantly exhorted to attend to the child's needs, interests, and abilities, it is no doubt useful for teachers to be acquainted with these general need systems. If a hierarchy concept has any validity, such knowledge is important because a child in the classroom may be attempting to satisfy some prepotent need when the teacher is attempting to activate the desire to know and understand. (p. 355)

Abraham Maslow (1943), the distinguished psychologist, proposed a theory of motivation based on human needs. Maslow viewed human needs in relationship to others and in a bottom-to-top hierarchy. He theorized that one need monopolizes a person's attention until that need is satisfied. His hierarchy of needs had five levels: physiological, safety, love and belonging, self-esteem, and self-actualization. Maslow's levels and descriptors for each are presented in Figure 2.2. The increase of cognitive abilities occurs in the self-actualization stage; however, if needs are largely unmet in other stages it is unlikely that much success in the cognitive area can be achieved, since these needs are both interrelated and interdependent. Instructional goals will not be fully realized without proper attention to student needs. Furthermore, the fundamental, lower-order needs must be met before teachers can be successful. Before a teacher can focus on a student's self-esteem, the student's physiological and safety needs must first be met. If a student's self-esteem is low, it is unlikely he or she will be motivated to try new things in the classroom. Likewise, if a student is hungry or tired, it is unlikely the student will want to learn or perhaps be able to learn, even if it will help him or her in next year's math class. The key at the self-esteem level, however, is to emphasize competency, that is, that your students are doing the right things and can be successful in your classroom. In addition to differences between prepotent levels (that is, levels of dominant or influential needs), differences exist within each level. For example, being successful in reading a social studies text is dependent not just on a student's general reading ability, but also on many instructional factors, including the readability level of the text and the application of specific skills such as ability to locate the main idea, significant details, sequence of events, and cause and effect relationships. The teacher's ability to enlist student interest and motivation in reading a particular chapter will also affect the student's level of success. This exemplifies the importance of the teacher and the teacher's influence in meeting or not meeting students' needs. By ascertaining that students have the prerequisite abilities to read a particular social studies chapter, the teacher can fulfill their instructional needs and help them succeed at the next learning task. In this view, one of the best ways to meet students' needs is to offer a sound instructional program. There is no substitute or commercial material to replace good teaching, which provides the bridge between basic student needs and instructional needs. Combs (1982) stresses the importance of meeting personal needs in the learning process. However, he goes on to place student needs in a wider perspective:

> That good teaching begins with helping students fulfill basic needs does not mean good teaching stops there. . . . It is not enough to simply satisfy student needs. The genius of good teaching lies in helping students discover needs they never knew they had. The most effective schools and teachers do more than satisfy existing student needs; they turn students on. They help students perceive ever broader horizons and greater depths of experience. (p. 29)

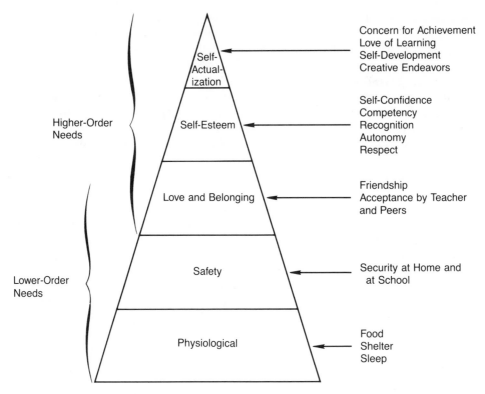

FIGURE 2.2 *Maslow's hierarchy of human needs*

Emotional Maturity

Everyone has emotional needs, and they play an important role in the learning process. Raths (1972) hypothesized that students have eight emotional needs: belonging, achievement, economic security, love and affection, sharing and respect, to be free from fear, to be free from intense feelings of guilt, and the need for self-concept and understanding. Students grow in a number of ways, including in emotional stability. If our needs are met, we feel good about ourselves and approach new events with confidence; conversely, if emotional needs are unmet, Raths hypothesized, this will lead to negative self-esteem and reluctance about and apathy toward undertaking new situations. Thus our emotions can be manifested in positive and negative ways. Combs (1983), speaking of emotion in a psychological sense, stated: "Emotion is understood as a state of readiness or acceleration." Depending upon our perception of a certain event as being satisfying or threatening or of little consequence, we express different levels and types of emotion.

Students who are emotionally mature handle new situations, periods of frustration, and stress with appropriate reactions. At such times a teacher might say that a certain student is motivated and giving great effort to an activity. It is certainly desirous to have students who cannot wait to get started on an activity and perform beyond minimum expectations. On the other hand, students who are not emotionally secure may respond to a given situation with aggression, hostility, withdrawal, or other compensating behavior. Such behaviors are considered symptoms of emotional needs. Since a student's emotional behavior influences learning, it is crucial for teachers to be aware of these emotional needs and create a classroom environment that promotes each student's emotional growth. Because each student has different needs it is imperative that individual differences be recognized and treated accordingly. For example, one student may thrive on an activity that is beyond his or her level, but that same activity may devastate another student of similar ability. Likewise a student may have a great emotional need to be a member of a group. If the teacher utilizes various grouping plans to involve this student continually with his or her classmates, greater learning and emotional growth can be attained.

Your daily interactions with your students and the classroom environment you create are the keys to promoting their emotional maturity. Your sensitivity toward students will directly affect their emotional growth as well as their cognitive growth. Being able to respond appropriately to them depends on how well you know them, how sensitive you are to their needs, and how able you are to "read" students. Combs, Blume, Newman, and Wass (1974) feel one characteristic of good teachers is a sensitivity to others. Describing the term, the authors wrote:

> Sensitivity is a matter of feelings, beliefs, and understandings, the ability to put oneself in the other fellow's shoes and to see the way things are with him. It is a matter of making inferences about how people think and feel and perceive and of checking these inferences against experience. (p. 73)

Therefore, your ability to understand students is dependent upon knowing them—not just academically but being acquainted with their interests, needs, likes, dislikes, health, fears, hobbies, and friends. Knowing the students will enable you to respond appropriately in various classroom situations. Being sensitive to the emotional needs of students will create a climate of acceptance and trust in which learning can flourish. Raths (1969) has listed a number of practical guidelines to foster students' emotional security in the learning situation:

> The teacher's behavior must be highly consistent.
> Children need to know the limits of acceptable behavior.
> Students need to feel physically secure.
> Every student feels more secure if he knows that the teacher will not diminish his status in the presence of his peers.
> Students want a teacher who can save them from extremes of humiliation.
> Students feel more secure when the teacher is relaxed and pleasant.
> Students feel more secure when the teacher's explanations, directions, and comments are clear and to the point.

Students feel more secure when they are with a teacher whom they consider to be fair.

Students feel more emotionally secure when they are respected.

Students feel more secure where there is a relative absence of fear.

Students feel much more secure when they believe that their teacher is loyal to them.

Students feel more secure when school becomes a place they can "live," not a place where they must serve time. (pp. 73–75)

Motivating Students to Learn

Teachers have always recognized the importance of motivation in the learning process. In fact, good instruction and motivation go hand in hand. A good job of motivation rarely occurs in isolation but is a part of instruction. To make learning alive and exciting, teachers must strive to make their instruction alive and exciting. Effective teachers at all grade levels, recognizing this close relationship, interweave motivation with instructional strategies throughout their day to meet student needs. Figure 2.3 displays the teaching-learning process and highlights the interrelationship between the concern for cognitive goals and the concern for affect. Essential elements in the teaching process for cognitive ends include diagnosis of student strengths and weaknesses, selection of appropriate learning goals, and actual instruction including motivation, presentation, practice, and evaluation. The fundamental concerns for student affect include self-perceptions, emotional maturity, and motivation. As depicted, the two triangles merge, with a simultaneous connection for learning cognitive goals and affect. The figure graphically demonstrates the pervasive concern for student affect in the achievement of cognitive goals that is involved in teaching.

What is motivation? What causes one student to want to go beyond the regular expectations and do more? Clearly, we all work harder in those areas we enjoy and in which we are successful. If we perceive the importance of a given task

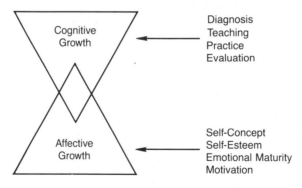

FIGURE 2.3 *Teaching-learning process*

and if conditions are such that we can be successful, our motivation is high. Good and Brophy (1977) have described motivation as "the level of task involvement and persistence that students exhibit, regardless of who designs or sets the task" (p. 377). The concept of motivation is complicated, since there are a variety of expert opinions concerning human interaction and many theories of motivation. We have found that some students are motivated to learn by the careful sequencing of activities to ensure success on a task and by the use of praise and reward systems; others are motivated to learn by a more intrinsic approach that focuses on the value of knowing, feelings, and interests. Since one strategy may work with one student but not with another, effective teachers implement different methods to motivate their students, monitor student reactions, and adjust future instruction accordingly. Though there is no one formula for motivating students, it is important to have a pervasive concern for motivating students throughout the day. Thus, teachers use different strategies to engage their students in learning depending upon the students themselves, what is being taught, and the classroom environment.

For a multitude of reasons, some students in any school system are not ready participants in the teaching-learning process. Teachers are constantly reminded to "motivate" these students. However, a step-by-step prescription for motivation for all students in all situations does not exist. Even so, a foundation of basic principles based on current research on motivation does exist for teachers to use. Two important generalizations should guide teachers' thinking on motivating students. First, a self-monitoring attitude should be adopted because of the individual nature of motivation, with one strategy working for a particular student at one time and not at another time. Second, teachers are in direct control of the motivational strategies in their classrooms. If you set a goal to promote a positive motivational climate in the classroom, chances are excellent you will achieve this goal. You as the teacher are in charge of the type of motivation that is used in the class. Regardless of where you teach and the previous problems of certain students, what you do in the classroom can directly affect how students feel. Thus, it is your responsibility and your challenge to enhance your students' self-concept and self-esteem and to create conditions throughout the day that ensure that your students experience success. Good and Brophy (1977) have examined the complex area of student motivation and concluded that teachers have at their disposal four basic methods to motivate students:

1. Change the task at hand.
2. Change how students perceive the learning task.
3. Vary the student-teacher relationship.
4. Change the reward structure in use in the classroom.

With these four methods as guideposts, I will recommend specific strategies under each to guide your emphasis on motivation in the classroom. I recommend that you pick and choose strategies depending on your specific situation to create an environment in which a high level of motivation can be maintained in the classroom.

Changing the Task: Practical Tips
- Match your instructional goals to the needs of the students.
- Match the difficulty level of your presentation to the cognitive levels of students.
- Capitalize upon the interests, background, experience, and cultures of your students in your presentation and selection of materials.
- Change the "scenery": Use different types of materials (commercial, teacher-made, programmed, educational games). Use different modes of presentation. Make use of different forms of feedback (verbal, written, group). Vary the pace of your lessons. Use different types of seatwork assignments. Vary the amount of time students can spend on an activity. Vary your record-keeping scheme to include student input. Use different types of groups (individual, small group, interest, research, partner, ability, and whole group). Periodically change the room arrangement to make learning more pleasurable.
- At times, provide students with a choice of materials to work with or books to read or ask for their input about the sequence of materials to be read to reach a given learning goal.
- When appropriate, structure lessons so that students can be active in the classroom.

Changing the Student's Perception of the Importance of the Task: Practical Tips
- Show enthusiasm for your subject and let students see your emotional responses—laughter or dissent, for example.
- Tell students how learning a particular skill will enable them to become more independent.
- Use graphic illustrations of their progress to show students they are improving.
- Continually tell students why they are doing what they are doing.
- Remind students in individual conferences that they will learn and be successful in your class (regardless of previous problems).
- Provide many varied opportunities for students to experience success.
- Allow students to rate stories and activities on a scale of 1 to 10 in order to show them that their opinion is valued.

Varying the Student-Teacher Relationship: Practical Tips
- Learn the interests of your students.
- Make it a point to communicate on a personal note with students whenever possible.
- Communicate with parents to learn more about students.
- Provide opportunities for students to interact with you about important learnings in the class.

- Encourage students to try, even if they fail at first.
- Cooperatively plan learning activities with students.

Changing the Reward Structure: Practical Tips
- In keeping with the instructional goal, use different materials on the same topic to ensure all students have a chance of success.
- Give a grade for effort in addition to the regular performance grade.
- Use cooperative learning groups (see FYI in this chapter) to raise students' chances of success and their perceptions of the importance of success. Form small groups composed of students of differing ability levels. Provide the group with an instructional goal that is to be reached as a group. Reward the quality of the group work with a group grade, so that students sink or swim together.

Interpersonal Skills

The ability to enhance the emotions of students will be directly related to developing good interpersonal relationships with them. To be successful in interpersonal relationships, a teacher needs to have a genuine concern for students' self-esteem and demonstrate effective communication skills. It is during classroom interactions that students' feelings are shaped and formulated. Students need to feel comfortable and accepted in order for them to be challenged to learn and be successful. The ways you react to students will go a long way toward enhancing or negating their self-esteem. Teachers who treat students fairly and speak to them in a respectful manner are practicing effective interpersonal skills. In this way, the concern for student self-esteem is linked to effective communication skills. Open communication is essential to help students learn. As a teacher, you need to be sensitive to cultivating communication skills and to monitoring the quality of your interactions with students. Among the communication skills you will want to refine are the ability to listen, skill at communicating positive and realistic expectations to your students, the ability to sustain productive discussions with students, and the ability to provide valuable feedback.

Unfortunately, teachers generally do most of the talking in classrooms, and students generally do most of the listening. Perhaps because of this, teachers sometimes do not really listen to what their students are saying or not saying. First, teachers need to provide themselves with more opportunities to listen to their students. Invite your students to give their opinions on a topic or to expand on their answers; respond to their ideas by probing further or summarizing their thoughts. By doing so, your actions will be telling them that what they have to say is valued. You will be creating an open environment in which they know you care because you listen. Your ability to communicate positive yet realistic expectations to students is crucial for learning. Chapter Eight deals entirely with this topic. Telling students they are capable and will learn in your classroom is essential. Your ability to sustain discussions with students is dependent upon communicating the idea that it is all right to try even if they respond incorrectly. Students need to feel supported by their teacher and to feel their input is valued and needed for the success of the lesson. Also, it is important to explain ideas clearly to students and to make certain that they understand what is said. This brings us to the topic of providing feedback to students. Effective feedback should be immediate and related to the task at hand, and it serves two purposes:

1. It gives you the opportunity to reinforce student learning.
2. It gives students a "shot in the arm" and a reason to continue to be involved in the lesson.

A longer treatment of the discussion-feedback cycle will be given in Chapter Four. The overriding principle is to involve all students in a supportive atmosphere.

SELF-MONITORING FYI

"Reading" Students

Definition: Inferring students' motivations, interests, and needs through the accumulation of information.

Indicators:
- Listen and evaluate your students' verbal responses for signs of hesitation, confusion, acceptance, self-confidence, motivation, interest, antagonism, and boredom.
- Be sensitive to nonverbal cues, for example, facial expressions, physical movements, reactions to peers, and reactions to failure.
- Know students' present level of achievement and specific instructional deficiencies.
- Know students' interests and be aware of their backgrounds.
- Look for patterns of student responses—always missing the main idea, for instance.
- Notice the students' preferences in activities or organizational patterns.
- Translate informed hunches into classroom action, that is, by making changes in instructional program.

SELF-MONITORING FYI

Cooperative Grouping

One way to increase student interaction and participation is to design cooperative learning experiences. In this type of grouping, the teacher forms groups of three to six students of different ability levels to work on an assignment. The teacher sets a group goal and rewards students depending on how well the group succeeds on a posttest. Members of the cooperative group have a vested interest in each other's progress, and student communication and sharing are emphasized. There is a growing body of research demonstrating the effectiveness of cooperating grouping procedures on both achievement and attitudes (Slavin, 1980). Although you can implement cooperative grouping in the elementary or secondary class in a variety of ways using your own materials, you can find descriptions of two cooperative grouping plans in Johnson and Johnson (1975) and DeVries and Slavin (1978). The basic steps for initiating cooperative groups are

- communicate the group instructional goal
- assign students of differing abilities (high, middle, low) to cooperative groups
- explain the activities and materials
- communicate the group evaluation procedure
- allow sufficient time for students to work together in their groups on the assignment (perhaps over several days)
- evaluate the instructional goal(s).

READER INTERACTION 1

Student Affect

Rationale and Directions: To gain insights into the feelings and emotions of students at the grade level you intend to teach, use the following questions to interview one or two teachers in your school.

1. What are the dominant attitudes and feelings students have in your grade level (needs, emotions, fears, likes, dislikes, values)?

2. Unfortunately, some students have had early experiences that have not been good. What are the main problems students have in your grade level?

3. What are some ways that you use to enhance students' self-esteem?

4. What strategies do you use to motivate students to learn?

SELF-MONITORING CRITIQUE

1. What are some ways in which you have balanced concerns for student feelings and for cognitive goals in your classroom? Were your methods effective? Ineffective? Why?

2. Relating back to Westbury's constraints in Chapter One, do you feel that a concern for student affect can hurt your ability to cover a sufficient number of topics in your classroom? Can it hurt your ability to ensure student mastery of material? Can it hurt your ability to have few problems in the area of discipline?

   Can a teacher overemphasize a concern for student affect?

3. What motivational strategies work best for you? Why do they work?

Summary

A concern for student feelings and emotions in the teaching-learning process was highlighted. The teacher effectiveness literature stresses instructional strategies and time usage, but it is mandatory to remember this effective instruction occurs in a warm, positive atmosphere. The best instruction takes place when there is an appropriate blend of a concern for mastery of learning objectives and a concomitant emphasis on student attitudes. To this end, teachers are encouraged to be sensitive and to attend to the following areas:

Self-perceptions—working to improve both the self-concept and the self-esteem of students.

Student needs—taking into account the needs of students using Maslow's need hierarchy as a reference point.

Emotional maturity—promoting a classroom climate of trust and acceptance.

Student motivation—designing successful learning experiences by changing the task, student perceptions of the task, student-teacher relationship, and the classroom reward structure.

References

Ausubel, D. P., & Robinson, F. G. (1969). *School learning: An introduction to educational psychology.* New York: Holt, Rinehart & Winston.

Beane, J. A., & Lipka, R. P. (1986). *Self-concept, self-esteem, and the curriculum.* New York: Teachers College.

Combs, A. W. (1982). *A personal approach to teaching: Beliefs that make a difference.* Boston: Allyn & Bacon.

Combs, A. W., Blume, R. A., Newman, A. J., & Wass, H. L. (1974). *The professional education of teachers* (2nd ed.). Boston: Allyn & Bacon.

DeVries, D., & Slavin, R. (1978). Teams—games—tournaments (TGT): Review of ten classroom experiments. *Journal of Research and Development in Education, 12,* 28–38.

Gambrell, L. B., & Wilson, R. M. (1973). *Focusing on the strengths of children.* Belmont, CA: Fearon.

Good, T. L., & Brophy, J. E. (1977). *Educational psychology: A realistic approach.* New York: Holt, Rinehart & Winston.

Johnson, D., & Johnson, R. (1975). *Learning together and alone.* Englewood Cliffs, NJ: Prentice-Hall.

Maslow, A. H. (1943). A theory of human motivation. *The Psychological Review, 50,* 370–396.

Raths, L. E. (1969). *Teaching for learning.* Columbus, OH: Merrill.

Raths, L. E. (1972). *Meeting the needs of children: Creating trust and security.* Columbus, OH: Merrill.

Rogers, C. R. (1987). On the shoulders of giants. *The Educational Forum, 51,* 115–122.

Rubin, L. J. (1973). Schooling and life. In L. J. Rubin (Ed.), *Facts and feelings in the classroom.* New York: Viking Press.

Slavin, R. (1980). Cooperative learning. *Review of Educational Research, 50,* 317–343.

Principles of Instruction

- Cultivate student feelings and emotions.
- **Maintain effective classroom control.**
- Provide an appropriate balance between fostering direct learnings and inquiry abilities.
- Maximize the use of classroom time to teach students what they need to know.
- Diagnose student strengths and weaknesses and provide instruction based on student needs.
- Use a variety of materials to teach what the students need to know.
- Believe in your ability as a teacher to make a difference and convince students that they will learn.

CHAPTER 3

Classroom Management

Managing the Classroom

Research on teaching has clearly pointed to the teacher's role in improving education. As we shall see in later chapters, your thoughts, judgments, and actions related to teaching methods have a direct bearing on whether or not students are provided an appropriate education. However, you must design and employ effective teaching techniques not for one student exclusively, but for an entire class simultaneously. Thus, in addition to purely "instructional" concerns, you need to be able to create, manage, and maintain an environment conducive to learning. Studies of the concerns of experienced, first year, and student teachers singled out classroom management as one of the most difficult and stressful elements in teaching (Fuller, 1969; Griffin, 1983; Simon, 1984; Lasley, 1987). Teachers-in-training and first year teachers, especially, equated success with the ability to manage the classroom effectively.

Studies have shown that effective instructors are proficient in classroom organization and management (Rosenshine & Berliner, 1978). Although they are interrelated and interdependent, managerial abilities need to be differentiated from the instructional abilities of teachers. Weber (1977) defined class management in this fashion:

> that set of activities by which the teacher promotes appropriate student behavior and eliminates inappropriate student behavior, develops good interpersonal relationships and a positive socioemotional climate in the classroom, and establishes and maintains an effective and productive classroom organization. (p. 286)

A teacher may have highly developed instructional skills in the areas of planning, teaching, and evaluating but fail miserably in the classroom because of a lack of managerial skills. Of course the opposite can also be true: A teacher may be highly skilled in classroom management and organization but fail because of poorly developed instructional abilities. Expertise in both areas is required for successful teaching.

Managerial concerns address the need for teachers to provide and maintain classroom conditions conducive to student learning. One only has to observe for a short time in a classroom to have a healthy regard for effective classroom management. Some teachers run such smooth classrooms that you may think management is an innate trait. Clearly, it is not, and dealing appropriately with the wide range of student abilities and needs in a classroom is a challenge. As part of your teacher training program, you may have already completed a course on classroom management and studied approaches to classroom discipline. While it is not my intent to focus on a particular discipline method or philosophy, some of the major approaches are listed below. You are encouraged to become familiar with various approaches to help clarify your own philosophy concerning discipline.

Reality Therapy: Glasser, W. (1969) *Schools without failure.* New York: Harper & Row. Glasser, W. (1986). *Control theory in the classroom.* New York: Harper & Row.

Behavior Modification: Skinner, B. F. (1968). *The technology of teaching.* New York: Appleton-Century-Crofts.

Eclectic Discipline: Wolfgang, C., & Glickman, C. (1986). *Solving discipline problems.* Boston: Allyn & Bacon.

Dreikurs, R., & Cassel, P. (1972). *Discipline without tears.* New York: Hawthorn Books.

Gordon, T. (1974). *T.E.T. Teacher effectiveness training.* New York: David McKay.

Assertive Discipline: Canter, L., & Canter, M. (1976). *Assertive discipline: A take charge approach for today's educator.* Seal Beach, CA: Canter & Associates.

The recommendations that follow reflect an eclectic view, representing philosophies that range from an affective or personal-growth perspective to an ecological, environmental view to a behavioristic approach. Effective managers generally use a combination of approaches because they have adopted a problem-solving attitude toward management. The nature of individual differences precludes the pronouncement of "the one correct way" of managing the classroom. The goal is to set optimal conditions for learning, and there are a multitude of ways to achieve this end. The method you use will depend on the grade level taught, the students, the subject, and the type of learning you are addressing.

Elements of Successful Management

As you might suspect, successful classroom managers have relatively few discipline problems, because they put their efforts into preventing or reducing the likelihood of trouble occurring in their classrooms. Studies on teaching have identified the teacher's ability to find ways to keep students actively engaged in instructional activities as the key to successful classroom management (Brophy & Evertson, 1976). Overwhelming evidence points to three clusters of attributes as key elements in achieving the goal of effective classroom management (Brophy & Evertson, 1976; Kounin, 1970; Emmer & Evertson, 1980):

1. planning of activities
2. managing of group instruction
3. monitoring of student progress

There is a positive side to each of these elements: You, the teacher, have direct control over each of them. Through practice and self-monitoring of your growth in this area, therefore, you can continue to improve, lesson after lesson.

Planning of Activities

Effective teachers remember the adage that "an ounce of prevention is worth a pound of cure," and systematically prepare for the upcoming school year, planning in advance for individual lessons (Emmer et al., 1980). Good managers spend time before the school year begins collecting and organizing materials and planning activities to be used with their students. The better the preparation of materials and activities prior to actual teaching the more confidence you will have in daily interactions with students and the more you can concentrate on actual teaching. Gathering materials at the last minute will eventually wear both you and your students down. Also, prior to the beginning of school and certainly in the first month of school, you will need to collect as many diagnostic data on your students as possible to aid in highlighting strengths and weaknesses of students. This information will help you in planning effective instruction throughout the year. Both the collection of diagnostic data on students and the collection of materials and activities prior to the beginning of school are considered "preventive" management measures, because spending time on these areas will ensure more meaningful instruction tailored to students' needs and free you of the burden of deciding these matters the day before or "on the spot." Above all, the key to effective classroom management is prevention (Good & Brophy, 1984). Good and Brophy succinctly state: "The key to success lies in the things the teacher does ahead of time to create a good learning environment and a low potential for trouble" (p. 177).

Furthermore, good classroom managers spend time at the start of each school year discussing classroom rules and procedures with their students. Depending on their age and grade level, the rules and procedures can range from rules for lining up for lunch and movement within the room to discussion procedures to rules for the use of hall passes. Your expectations should be made clear to students, and it is best to model these behaviors with younger children. These rules and procedures need to be reviewed with all students until they know them. By ensuring that these procedures are clear to the students, you will be preventing possible management problems.

Management Suggestions to Consider in Your Preparation Before the School Year Begins
- Collect as many diagnostic data on students as possible.
- Decide on "must" classroom behavior rules and procedures (i.e., those not negotiable with students) regarding tardiness, dismissal, hall passes, makeup work, homework, and so forth.
- Decide ahead of time how you intend to explain classroom behavior standards and your expectations concerning assignments and classroom procedures.
- Organize and arrange instructional materials for easy access and distribution.
- Plan the seating arrangement to ensure a smooth transition of movement from one activity to another. You should be able to see the whole class from wherever you are stationed when teaching and you will need to monitor students during supervised and independent assignments.
- List rules and procedures on the board or on a bulletin board. Communicate to students the consequences of improper behavior.
- Check the class roster to determine if any special education students will be mainstreamed in your room.
- Prepare an introductory letter to parents explaining classroom policies.

Closer to the start of actual instruction, effective classroom managers plan their lessons well enough in advance to ensure that their students remain engaged in learning. This lesson planning should be detailed in your mind if not written down. Effective teachers "walk through" their lessons in their minds before teaching them in the classroom. Teachers need to review how the lesson will begin, what type of procedure will be followed, when and how materials will be distributed, what interaction patterns will be used with students, how students will complete seatwork assignments, how corrective feedback will be given, and how an activity will end and the next begin without chaos erupting. Incorrect timing of any of the above procedures can lead to students straying from the task at hand. For example, if you pass out materials for seatwork before they are to be used and then expect the students to listen to you, you will be fighting an uphill battle. This seemingly small matter can lead to big problems; unfortunately it is a common occurrence in many classrooms. Likewise, if you don't plan ahead for those students who finish their seatwork assignments sooner than others, you are asking for the normal flow of the lesson to be interrupted and possible problems to emerge.

Management Suggestions to Consider in Your Preparation to Teach a Lesson
- Have all materials and dittos run off and ready to use well in advance of the actual lesson.
- Decide on how and when materials will be used.
- Know when you will distribute materials to students. Be careful not to distribute materials at the wrong time.
- Plan more than one way to explain a particular concept to your students. Anticipate that some students will not understand after the first go-around.
- Think through your lesson to highlight times when students will be moving around the room. Plan ahead for smooth transitions.
- Plan how you will handle seatwork assignments—directions, manner of completion, collection of finished products, activities for those students who finish early—and how you intend to monitor student attention to the assignment.

Managing Group Instruction

Good classroom managers successfully orchestrate group instruction and attend to a multitude of human interactions that occur continuously throughout the day. Obviously, some teachers are more successful in managing groups of students day in and day out than others. What separates the more effective managers from the less effective? Successful classroom managers generally think ahead to avoid potential problems, sense the proper pace of a lesson, and have a continuous grasp of the total classroom situation. In addition, the work of Kounin (1970) identified several effective group techniques to ensure smooth running and productive instruction. These techniques can be planned to a certain degree, and they will help you deal effectively with group instruction. Kounin identified successful managers as possessing the following attributes: "withitness," overlapping, smoothness of transition, momentum, group alerting, and accountability. Here's what these terms mean.

- *Withitness* refers to a teacher's ability to be continuously aware of what's going on in the classroom and to communicate this awareness to students.
- *Overlapping* refers to a teacher's ability to do more than one thing at a time in the classroom without getting frustrated.
- *Smoothness of transitions* refers to the ability to go from one activity to another or one part of a lesson to another without wasting time and without undue delay.

- *Momentum* means the teacher's ability to pace lessons at a "just right" speed with few delays.
- *Group alerting* has to do with the teacher's ability to keep student attention during lessons.
- *Accountability* refers to the teacher's ability to know how well students are learning.

It does take time to develop these abilities; it doesn't just happen. However, you can develop these techniques: They are learned, not innate, traits. Successfully implementing these techniques relates directly to providing quality instructional time for your students.

Management Suggestions to Consider while Teaching a Lesson
- Remember to have the students' attention before you begin.
- Be sensitive to the correct timing of your explanation. Notice nonverbal cues from students that indicate interest or lack of interest.
- Watch students' eyes. They can indicate lack of understanding of or interest in what you are saying.
- Don't try to cover too much in a single lesson.
- Don't dwell too long on a topic or a response. On the other hand, do not leave a question hanging.
- Vary your questioning techniques depending on instructional goal (see Chapter Four).
- Enforce classroom rules fairly and consistently.
- Keep interruptions to a minimum.
- Anticipate problems and handle any misbehavior quickly and in as positive a manner as possible.
- Provide feedback to students that is related to the academic task at hand.
- Circulate around the room.

Monitoring Student Progress

Checking on how students are accomplishing instructional goals serves three purposes: (1) to tell you how well students are understanding new material; (2) to help you to focus your students' thinking on specific learnings; and (3) to serve to maintain an atmosphere conducive to learning. The effective monitoring of student progress offers a wonderful example of how management and instructional concerns are truly interdependent.

It would be ideal, of course, if students automatically mastered new learnings after an initial presentation or coverage by the teacher, but in reality, students need reinforcement and at times reteaching to learn new material. Therefore, teachers must keep an eye on student progress and be able to respond quickly and appropriately. One way to do so is to monitor classroom discussion and seatwork activities. Picking up on student needs at an early stage and responding effectively not only enhances student learning but prevents management problems. The specific nature of the feedback is important. A preponderance of negative feedback or of vague comments is not beneficial. As much as possible, you want to give task-related or academically focused feedback that is specific to the work at hand and redirects the student's thinking or helps to clarify a response. If a student is not completing his or her work as instructed, an example of a task-related comment would be, "John, we are working on pages 27 and 28 in your algebra book and we will go over the answers in fifteen minutes." If a student responds with an incomplete answer, a task-related comment might be, "You are on the right track, Jane, but can you tell me more regarding why the experiment did not work?" The more positive and specific the feedback is to the instructional goal and the expected response, the more students will learn, and the fewer the management problems will be.

The study of feedback that teachers provide to students, especially the use of praise, to reinforce and motivate their learning has been a topic of interest in the study of teaching (Brophy, 1981). Contrary to the popular belief that "you can't praise students enough," findings on the effectiveness of the use of praise by teachers have been mixed. Depending on the situation and the students, praise (too much or too little, or too general in nature) can negatively affect student learning. Praising one student in one way may be a positive reinforcer, but to another student that same praise might be a negative reinforcer. Overall, praise tends to be effective if it is directed specifically at what a student is doing. As you begin to teach, it is important to be aware of your use of praise and the effect of it on students. To help in monitoring your own progress in this area, Figure 3.1 contains guidelines for effective praise developed by Brophy (1981). These guidelines are aimed at using praise as a positive reinforcer and a vehicle to develop intrinsic student motivation.

Management Suggestions to Consider in Monitoring Student Progress
- Have students show their work to you.
- Have students demonstrate the particular skill or knowledge.
- Ask students directly how they are proceeding with the activity.
- Provide meaningful praise.
- Monitor seatwork activities by walking around the room and stopping to work with individual students on the assignment. Give immediate feedback.
- Give explicit direction for the seatwork activity or assignment. Go over the first two or three examples to be certain the students understand the task.
- Make expectations clear.
- Plan a variety of activities and assignments.
- Check for student understanding before going on to next major point.
- Have students work in teams of three or four and circulate among the teams to check progress.
- Be sensitive to signs of confusion—unnecessary movement or talking, puzzlement, lack of correct response to an easy question.

- Return student assignments with written feedback as quickly as possible.
- Have parents initial completed homework assignments.
- Be available to help students and to give positive feedback.
- Make sure seatwork assignments make sense to students. Ask them to state the purpose of the assignment.

Effective Praise	Ineffective Praise
1. is delivered contingently.	1. is delivered randomly or unsystematically.
2. specifies the particulars of the accomplishment.	2. is restricted to global positive reactions.
3. shows spontaneity, variety, and other signs of credibility; suggests clear attention to the student's accomplishment.	3. shows a bland uniformity which suggests a conditioned response made with minimal attention.
4. rewards attainment of specified performance criteria (which can include effort criteria, however).	4. rewards mere participation, without consideration of performance processes or outcomes.
5. provides information to students about their competence or the value of their accomplishments.	5. provides no information at all or gives students information about their status.
6. orients students toward better appreciation of their own task-related behavior and thinking about problem solving.	6. orients students toward comparing themselves with others and thinking about competing.
7. uses students' own prior accomplishments as the context for describing present accomplishments.	7. uses the accomplishments of peers as the context for describing students' present accomplishments.
8. is given in recognition of noteworthy effort or success at difficult (for *this* student) tasks.	8. is given without regard to the effort expended or the meaning of the accomplishment (for *this* student).

FIGURE 3.1 *Guidelines for effective praise (From "Teacher praise: A functional analysis" by Jere E. Brophy,* **Review of Educational Research,** *Spring 1981, pp. 5–32. Copyright 1981, American Educational Research Association, Washington, D.C. Reprinted by permission.)*

9. attributes success to effort and ability, implying that similar successes can be expected in the future.

9. attributes success to ability alone or to external factors such as luck or (easy) task difficulty.

10. fosters endogenous attributions (students believe that they expend effort on the task because they enjoy the task and/or want to develop task-relevant skills).

10. fosters exogenous attributions (students believe that they expend effort on the task for external reasons—to please the teacher, win a competition or reward, etc.).

11. focuses students' attention on their own task-relevant behavior.

11. focuses students' attention on the teacher as an external authority figure who is manipulating them.

12. fosters appreciation of, and desirable attributions about, task-relevant behavior after the process is complete.

12. intrudes into the ongoing process, distracting attention from task-relevant behavior.

FIGURE 3.1—*Continued*

Different Contexts

If the learning goal is student mastery of basic skills and knowledge, the effective manager takes direct control of the learning. The teacher formally explains what is to be learned in a group setting, keeps students working on academic activities by limiting discussion and student input, communicates directly and indirectly an awareness of what's going on, monitors student progress, and controls the pacing of the lesson. Though this sounds old fashioned and controlling, this "control" is maintained in a supportive atmosphere conducive to learning. Also, the effective manager is goal-driven. The controlling nature of this scenario is necessary to assure that available time for instruction is used properly. The major difference between this type of control and the use of negative reinforcers, of course, is that the atmosphere created by the teacher is pervasively positive. If you manage your class effectively but do so by using negative reinforcers, achievement can be adversely affected.

It is important to note that this style of management works best for teaching basic skills and knowledge in a subject area. For developing inquiry and thinking skills, however, less teacher control and more student choice and input are advantageous. Again, managerial concerns depend upon a host of variables. You must exercise sound professional judgment based on your own situation and instructional goals.

It is rather surprising to learn that studies of teacher effectiveness support small and large group instruction more than they do one-to-one instruction (McDonald, 1976). With respect to classroom management, instructing students in a group situation as opposed to letting individual students work on their own helps keep students attentive to the task at hand. If the situation is handled correctly, teachers can more easily attend to Westbury's constraints of mastery, coverage, affect, and discipline in a group situation. The recommendation to group students is another case of an "old" belief that is now supported by research. As with all recommended practices, effective grouping practices will vary depending on many factors, especially the type of learning objective pursued and the grade level of students. In kindergarten through grade three, the use of small groups is especially beneficial. Small groups coupled with a great deal of teacher feedback are needed for early success in reading and math. Small groups allow for instruction on youngsters' instructional or "just right" level. The use of large groups is conducive to learning basic skills and information in most school subjects in grades four through twelve. However, if critical thinking is the learning objective, less structure is required and a looser combination of small, large, and individual groupings is recommended.

The focus on prevention rather than correction in classroom management simply makes good sense. When teachers put in the time to plan all facets of their instruction ahead of time, it is reasonable to assume their efforts will pay off in school achievement. Although some may argue that emphasizing prevention belabors the obvious, many "obvious" propositions that were accepted through the ages have been found to be false when put to empirical tests. Furthermore, the notion of preventive classroom management strategies has the advantage that it can be used by teachers immediately. Teachers have direct control over initiating preventive strategies.

Personal Characteristics of Teachers

Personal characteristics will also affect how well you fare as a classroom manager. I do not mean to recommend that every teacher have the same personality, of course. Effective teachers certainly have different personalities. But, regardless of personality type, success with students will be linked to your genuinely liking students, enjoying teaching, treating students with fairness and respect, allowing students to feel at home in the classroom, and communicating concern for them. Successful teachers know their students, both personally and academically, and communicate this interest to them. Students should never feel they are merely computer ID numbers. Teachers who take the time to know their students are practicing preventive classroom management and will be more successful in their classroom teaching.

Stopping Misbehavior

Even in the best of classrooms, management problems still sometimes occur that require intervention by the teacher. The level of response can be viewed on a continuum from a nonverbal response to a simple reprimand to removal of a student(s) from the classroom (see Figure 3.2). There is no sure formula for handling management or discipline problems once they surface in the classroom. Knowing several possible means of dealing with student misconduct, however, will help you respond properly. Your response to a disturbance will depend upon your ability to prioritize the severity of the problem.

The keys to effective intervention are keeping your cool, avoiding extremely negative responses, responding (as the situation warrants) as quickly as possible, and being unafraid to ask for help from other professionals. Every teacher will have discipline problems, and you should realize that you are not expected to solve all problems by yourself. You are a member of a team that includes your principal, curriculum supervisor, social worker, guidance counselor, specialized teachers (reading, speech, special education), fellow classroom teachers, and parents. Don't be afraid to consult these people to help in correcting a problem.

During a lesson, your goal should be to develop a low-key style that will keep students working on their assignments. Losing your cool or giving an extremely negative response will probably undo any good previously accomplished. In addition, these actions have a widespread effect on other members of the class. This effect has been called the "ripple effect" by Kounin. He labels a teacher's responses to misbehavior as "desists." The use of negative desists or responses to misbehavior is especially counterproductive to a positive social and academic climate in the classroom. Desists that clearly identify the student, clearly communicate that the behavior is unacceptable, and clearly give the reason for the behavior being unacceptable are more effective than general reprimands.

Tied to prevention of management problems and handling of discipline problems is keeping lines of communication open with parents. There is also a ripple effect that goes on when contacting parents concerning a student's progress or lack of progress. Class rules and procedures should be clearly communicated to parents both in writing and in person. You will need the parents to support you throughout the year, and nothing helps build rapport with parents more than open communication, beginning from day one. In the event of an embarrassing situation or a discipline problem, it is essential that you inform parents. A crisis or potential problem is more easily solved if you have had previous communication with the parents.

SELF-MONITORING FYI

Pacing
Definition: The speed and coordination of your lesson.

Low	Moderate	High
Silence.	Change tone of voice.	Firmly inform student(s) of consequences of the action. Give ten seconds for student(s) to stop.
"Evil eye," icy stare.		
Physical proximity—move toward disruptive student while continuing on with lesson.	Isolate student from group for a short period of time.	
	Direct a task-related comment to the student(s).	Send for help if there is potential for physical violence.
Praise acceptable behavior of other students.	Remind students of certain class rules and procedures.	Keep other students away from disruptive student(s).
Remind students of your expectation for them in the activity at hand.	Walk over to student and quietly tell him/her that type of behavior is unacceptable and that working on assigned material is what should be done.	Remove student from class.
Remove materials a student is using for a short period of time.		Review incident with class and remind students of classroom rules and procedures.
	Direct a question to student regarding activity.	
	Take away student privileges.	
	Discuss problem with group.	
	Individually remind student that learning is his/her responsibility—not yours.	
	Contact parents.	
	Write up a contract and have student sign it.	

FIGURE 3.2 *Response to classroom disruptions*

Tips:

- Realize that even the best teachers can have lessons that are completed too slowly or too quickly. At times you want students to achieve so much that you try and cover too much in a short period of time. In such cases you might "finish" the lesson plan but not achieve your instructional goals; remember that tomorrow is another day.
- Have as your goal to progress at a speed that enables you to maintain student involvement and achieve instructional goals.
- Try to promote a coordinated effort. Moving too quickly or too slowly will make you and your students feel disjointed.
- Know students' learning needs and learning rates and be sensitive to signs of confusion or lackadaisical effort and then respond to these telltale signs by adapting your lesson. These are the keys to good pacing.

READER INTERACTION 2

Participation Guide
Directions:
1. Fill in the names of the students in your classroom in the seating chart on p. 45. Ask another student teacher or your cooperating teacher to complete this exercise for one of your lessons. At a later time, analyze the information collected by answering the summarizing and analyzing questions.
2. While sitting in the back of the room, the observer should put a check (✔) in the box for each student who answers a question.
3. Additionally, the observer should look around the room and eye each student for two or three seconds. Record a minus (-) for each student who exhibits inappropriate behavior (looking around the room when he or she should be listening to the teacher, talking to another student, writing when he or she should be listening). If a student is paying attention, do not place a mark of any kind in his or her box. The observer should look around the room every ten minutes, marking a student's block on the seating chart for inappropriate behavior.

Summarizing and Analyzing Questions
1. Which students answered more questions than others? List their names.

2. Were there students or groups of students not exhibiting appropriate behavior (looking around the room, talking to another student, writing when they should be listening?   yes   no

   If yes, list their names.

   Is there a relationship between your answers to questions 1 and 2? If so, what is the relationship?

3. If you had classroom disruptions, what type of response did you give (low, moderate, or high)?

   Was your response effective?

   Would you respond differently the next time this disruption occurs?

SEATING CHART

READER INTERACTION 3

Classroom Management Problems and Solutions

There are many effective techniques to handle a particular problem. List below the problem and the techniques employed to solve it. For example:

Problem: A student in the back of the room is talking.
Solution: The teacher walks to the back of the room, stands
   there for a few minutes, and continues the class discussion.

Observe or discuss classroom management problems and solutions with other students, cooperating teacher, or university supervisor.

Problem:

Solution:

Problem:

Solution:

SELF-MONITORING CRITIQUE

1. What techniques work best for you in maintaining student attention during group instruction?

2. Are there times when it is best to ignore some misbehavior?

3. Relating back to Westbury's four constraints in Chapter One, is it possible to overemphasize a concern for discipline?

   If so, how?

4. Do you use praise as a reinforcer in your classroom? How? Can you think of times when the use of praise was beneficial and when it was not?

Summary

The pressing need to manage the classroom effectively was the focus of this chapter. Creating and maintaining an atmosphere conducive to learning require teachers to practice "preventive" classroom management techniques. The following three elements from the teacher effectiveness research were discussed:

> *Planning of activities—long- and short-term thinking regarding the classroom environment, materials, instructional goals, and students.*

> *Managing group instruction*—thinking ahead regarding ways to ensure smoothly flowing lessons (Kounin's techniques of withitness, overlapping, smoothness of transitions, momentum, group alerting, and accountability).
> *Monitoring student progress*—systematically checking student progress in fulfillment of instructional goals.

Though the emphasis should be on prevention rather than correction, all teachers will have to deal with student misbehavior. A strategy based on prioritizing the severity of the problem and on using as low-key a response as possible was recommended.

References

Brophy, J. (1981). Teacher praise: A functional analyses. *Review of Educational Research, 51,* 5–32. (ERIC No. EJ 246 420)

Brophy, J., & Evertson, C. (1976). *Learning from teaching: A developmental perspective.* Boston: Allyn & Bacon.

Emmer, E. T., & Evertson, C. M. (1980). Synthesis of research on classroom management. *Educational Leadership, 38,* 342–347.

Emmer, E. T., Evertson, C. M., & Anderson, L. M. (1980). Effective classroom management at the beginning of the school year. *Elementary School Journal, 80,* 219–231.

Fuller, F. (1969). Concerns of teachers. *American Educational Research Journal, 6,* 207–226.

Good, T., & Brophy, J. (1984). *Looking in classrooms* (3rd ed.). New York: Harper & Row.

Griffin, G. A. (1983). *Student teaching and the commonplaces of schooling.* Austin, TX: Research and Development Center for Teacher Education. Report No. 9038.

Kounin, J. S. (1970). *Discipline and group management in classrooms.* New York: Holt, Rinehart & Winston.

Lasley, T. J. (1987). Classroom management. *The Educational Forum, 51,* 285–298.

McDonald, F. I. (1976). *Beginning teacher evaluation study, Phase II summary.* Princeton, NJ: Educational Testing Service.

Rosenshine B., & Berliner, D. (1978). Academic engaged time. *British Journal of Teacher Education, 4,* 3–16.

Simon, V. (1984). Perceived problems of beginning teachers. *Review of Educational Research, 54,* 143–178.

Weber, W. A. (1977). Classroom management. In Cooper, J. M., Hansen, J., Martorella, P. H., Morine-Dershimer, G., Sedker, D., Sadker, M., Sokolove, S., Shostak, R., TenBrink, T., and Weber, W. A., *Classroom teaching skills: A handbook.* Lexington, MA: D. C. Heath.

Principles of Instruction

- Cultivate student feelings and emotions.
- Maintain effective classroom control.
- **Provide an appropriate balance between fostering direct learnings and inquiry abilities.**
- Maximize the use of classroom time to teach students what they need to know.
- Diagnose student strengths and weaknesses and provide instruction based on student needs.
- Use a variety of materials to teach what the students need to know.
- Believe in your ability as a teacher to make a difference and convince students that they will learn.

CHAPTER 4

Differentiated Instruction

Types of Learnings

Differentiated instruction is instruction modified to suit student strengths and weaknesses and to suit an intended instructional goal. If all instruction could be the same for all students in each grade, teaching would be easy. The complexity of teaching is quickly realized when one tries to differentiate one's instruction according to student needs and the content to be taught.

As you begin to observe and teach individual lessons, you will find that some learning outcomes are specific or direct and some are open-ended or indirect. Basically, subjects and important skills within each subject involve two broad types of learnings: direct and inquiry. What I call direct learnings are sometimes referred to as explicit, systematic, or structured, depending on the author. These learnings are amenable to specific learning objectives in which observable student behavior can be verified using criterion-referenced or standardized tests. Inquiry learnings are learnings in which to have specific objectives is impractical and virtually impossible. Other terms synonymous with inquiry are asystematic, indirect, implicit, informal, and unstructured. Some examples of lesson objectives for direct and inquiry learnings are given below.

Direct:
Given a list of geometric figures following instruction, all students will be
  able to calculate the perimeter of the figures in centimeters 100 percent of
  the time.
Given a list of French words following instruction, all students will spell at
  least 90 percent of the words correctly.

Inquiry:

Students will be able to name their favorite poem by Browning and relate what it means to them.

Following a discussion and a film on Third World countries, students will have a better understanding of the freedoms they enjoy in the United States.

As you can see, direct learning objectives specify a goal in terms of observable student behavior and a quantifiable competency level. In the case of inquiry learning, objectives can be delineated but are more general in nature. Both types of learnings are essential in all subject areas. It is perfectly acceptable to teach a lesson and not be able to write a very specific or behavioral objective for the lesson's goal. Both styles of instruction are important, and a healthy balance should be struck between the two in planning your lessons. Reliance on one or the other can be counterproductive in the long run. For example, teaching exclusively for students to pass a basic skills test in reading comprehension may result in improved test scores; if you do so, however, the students will probably be unable to respond to critical thinking questions from their reading. Also, relying only on higher-level thinking will not produce the intended benefits if students are not in command of the facts that they need for this type of thinking. In addition to recognizing the importance of both types of learnings in each subject area, you should also realize that neither type of learnings is taught in the same way.

Direct Learnings

From research on teaching there has emerged a set of procedures that are effective in teaching a body of knowledge to students. Of course, you will need to modify any set of procedures according to your students, their grade and age, their readiness for a particular skill, and the subject. Acknowledging this limitation, however, does not diminish the importance of the six instructional functions delineated by Rosenshine and Stevens (1986) (see Figure 4.1). Teachers who use these procedures consistently produce higher than average achievement in their classes. Obviously, a lesson will not contain each aspect of all functions as listed. Rather, the lesson should employ each function to the degree that the students' abilities and needs demand at a given time. It is important to reiterate that these teaching procedures have been found effective in teaching systematic, direct, or structured knowledge and skills in school subjects, that is, in direct instruction. At the heart of this process is the direct explanation and demonstration of a given skill by the teacher. Direct learnings can be broken down into a series of parts. The teacher explains the task at hand in small steps using examples and counterexamples. This can be accomplished through the inductive or discovery process or the deductive process. In the inductive process the teacher leads the students to discover the skill by questioning them using examples and counterexamples. The

1. Daily Review and Checking Homework

   Checking homework (routine for students to check each other's papers)

   Reteaching when necessary

   Reviewing relevant past learning (may include questioning)

   Review prerequisite skills (if applicable)

2. Presentation

   Provide short statement of objectives

   Provide overview and structuring

   Proceed in small steps but at a rapid pace

   Intersperse questions within the demonstration to check for understanding

   Highlight main points

   Provide sufficient illustrations and concrete examples

   Provide demonstrations and models

   When necessary, give detailed and redundant instructions and examples

3. Guided Practice

   Initial student practice takes place with teacher guidance

   High frequency of questions and overt student practice (from teacher and/or materials)

   Questions are directly relevant to the new content or skill

   Teacher checks for understanding (CFU) by evaluating student responses

   During CFU teacher gives additional explanation, process feed-back, or repeats explanation—where necessary

   All students have a chance to respond and receive feedback; teacher insures that all students participate

   Prompts are provided during guided practice (where appropriate)

   Initial student practice is sufficient so that students can work independently

   Guided practice continues until students are firm

   Guided practice is continued (usually) until a success rate of 80% is achieved

FIGURE 4.1 *Instructional Functions*
(From "Teaching Functions" by B. Rosenshine and R. Stevens, in **Handbook of Research on Teaching** *[pp. 377–391] edited by M. C. Wittrock, 1986, New York: Macmillan. Copyright 1986 by the American Educational Research Association. Reprinted by permission.)*

4. Correctives and Feedback

Quick, firm, and correct responses can be followed by another question or short acknowledgement of correctness (i.e., "That's right")

Hesitant correct answers might be followed by process feedback (i.e., "Yes, Linda, that's right because . . .")

Student errors indicate a need for more practice

Monitor students for systematic errors

Try to obtain a substantive response to each question

Corrections can include sustaining feedback (i.e., simplifying the question, giving clues), explaining, reviewing steps, giving process feedback, or reteaching the last steps

Try to elicit an improved response when the first one is incorrect

Guided practice and corrections continue until the teacher feels that the group can meet the objectives of the lesson

Praise should be used in moderation, and specific praise is more effective than general praise.

5. Independent Practice (Seatwork)

Sufficient practice

Practice is directly relevant to skills/content taught

Practice to overlearning

Practice until responses are firm, quick, and automatic

Ninety-five percent correct rate during independent practice

Students alerted that seatwork will be checked

Student held accountable for seatwork

Actively supervise students, when possible

6. Weekly and Monthly Reviews

Systematic review of previously learned material

Include review in homework

Frequent tests

Reteaching of material missed in tests

Note: With older, more mature learners, or learners with more knowledge of the subject, the following adjustments can be made: (1) the size of the step in presentation can be larger (more material is presented at one time), (2) there is less time spent on teacher-guided practice and (3) the amount of overt practice can be decreased, replacing it with covert rehearsal, restating and reviewing.

FIGURE 4.1—*Continued*

deductive process begins with the teacher telling the students what the knowledge or skill is and then using examples to support the definition. Both the inductive and deductive methods of explaining new knowledge and skills are effective; the choice of one over the other is a matter of style taking into consideration the learning objective and students. The second major part of this process is teacher-supervised practice. Succinctly, this means that the teacher completes a few problems or examples with the students to make sure they understood the teacher's initial explanations. This is followed by independent practice to ensure that the students master the particular skill. The key to this process is student involvement with the teacher. Teachers who command the attention of their students while teaching direct learnings are more likely to have students learn than those who do not. This direct instruction procedure promotes the productive use of classroom time and student learning.

Inquiry Learnings

As we know, teaching does not just involve ensuring that students can adequately handle structured or explicit knowledge in a particular subject area. Clearly these learnings are important and are assessed on basic skill tests and various standardized tests. Effective teaching also involves teaching students to think critically and creatively. This requires a different style of teaching from that used for direct learning. Both styles are absolutely necessary. Addressing this issue, Rosenshine and Stevens state:

> These explicit teaching procedures are most applicable in those areas where the objective is to master a body of knowledge or learn a skill which can be taught in a step-by-step manner. Thus, these procedures apply to the teaching of facts that students are expected to master so that they can be used with new information in the future. Examples include arithmetic facts, decoding procedures, vocabulary, musical notation, English grammar, the factual parts of science and history, the vocabulary and grammar of foreign languages, and the factual and explicit parts of electronics, cooking, and accounting.
>
> Similarly, these procedures apply to the teaching of processes or skills that students are expected to apply to new problems or situations. This includes mathematical computation, blending sounds in decoding, map reading, the mechanics of writing personal and business letters, English grammar, applying scientific laws, solving algebraic equations, or tuning an automobile engine. In these cases, the student is taught a general rule which is then applied to new situations. (p. 377)

The authors also state these procedures are "least applicable for teaching in areas which are 'ill-structured,' that is, where the skills to be taught do not follow explicit steps . . . teaching composition and writing of term papers, analyses of literature, problem solving in specific content areas, discussion of social issues, or the development of unique or creative responses" (p. 377). Unfortunately, the literature on teaching has concentrated on the teaching of specific content and skills assessable on tests (direct learnings). However, some concurrence is beginning to emerge on the indicators of effective teaching of inquiry objectives. Student learning of critical and creative processes tends to be successful when the classroom teacher sets aside time for students to engage in thinking activities. The message is clear: if students are not asked to think, they will not do so. The simple matter of allocated time is vital to developing inquiry abilities. With the pressure to have students pass state-mandated literacy exams, many teachers do not allot time for any objectives other than those assessed on the state exams. Most of the learning assessed on these exams is systematic or direct in nature. Thus, students are not given the opportunity to think on higher levels. The current definition of basic skills unfortunately does not include the ability to think on higher levels. Both types of learning are "basic skills," and both should receive adequate attention in our schools. Also, each type of learning contributes strongly to the other. A literate person possesses both facts and understandings and is able to use information to analyze and think divergently. A good thing to realize is that you will have control over whether you allocate time for inquiry activities, that is, over whether you allow students to think or not. An excellent text on teaching thinking skills is by Raths et al. (1966, 1986). In this classic text, the authors postulate a positive relationship between an emphasis on thinking skills in the classroom and student behavior. The text is a helpful source for numerous practical activities that teachers can use to develop thinking skills at all grade levels and in every subject.

Is mere exposure to thinking activities enough to foster higher-level thinking? To a small degree, it may be, but students must be given an explanation of the inquiry skill and guidance in its development. However, this "direct explanation" is different in nature from the direct instruction model. It is important to remember that the initial learning of a particular inquiry skill (for example, how to judge reasonableness and relevancy of information or how to go about planning a trip to Egypt) will require an explanation of that skill. It is the practice (both supervised and independent), however, that is treated differently. The underlying difference is in pacing and control. In the teaching of direct learnings, the teacher is always in direct control of the learning. In teaching an inquiry skill, though, the teacher assumes the role of facilitator. Even so, the teacher must communicate the purpose of the inquiry skill and its relevance to students, bring prior experiences to bear on the current issue, use clear and relevant examples in discussing the process, provide occasional summaries of main points, use task-related comments and probing questions to clarify points, involve as many students as possible in discussions, and be ready to reteach or offer alternative explanations depending on student understanding. However, the time given to independent learning of an inquiry ability is more extensive and greater student interaction is recommended. Different grouping procedures can be used—research, interest, partner, cooperative—to a greater degree to allow students the opportunity to collect data on a topic, analyze and synthesize the information, and react to and report their

Direct = *   Inquiry = X

TEACHER CONTROL OF THE CLASS

No Control   Firm

			X		*	
1	2	3	4	5	6	7

WHO DIRECTS THE LEARNING?

Teacher   Students

*				X		
1	2	3	4	5	6	7

AMOUNT OF STUDENT MOVEMENT IN CLASS

None   Much

	*				X	
1	2	3	4	5	6	7

SOCIAL INTERACTION

None   Much

	*				X	
1	2	3	4	5	6	7

WHO CONTROLS THE PACING OF INSTRUCTION?

Teacher   Students

*					X	
1	2	3	4	5	6	7

NOISE IN THE CLASSROOM

Very Noisy   Silence

			X		*	
1	2	3	4	5	6	7

WHO DECIDES WHAT THE INSTRUCTIONAL ACTIVITIES WILL BE?

Teacher   Students

*			X			
1	2	3	4	5	6	7

FIGURE 4.2 *Direct Versus Inquiry Instruction*

Direct = *   Inquiry = X

AMOUNT OF INDEPENDENT PRACTICE

None						Much
		*			X	
1	2	3	4	5	6	7

MONITORING OF STUDENT PROGRESS

None						Much
			X			*
1	2	3	4	5	6	7

LEVEL OF COMPREHENSION QUESTIONS

Exclusively Factual						Exclusively Critical
	*			X		
1	2	3	4	5	6	7

FIGURE 4.2—*Continued*

findings. Figure 4.2 summarizes the major differences between direct and inquiry instruction.

The Planning Process

Good instruction doesn't "just happen" in the classroom but is the result of much teacher effort before the students arrive at school. Your skill at planning will greatly affect both your success as a teacher and your students' learning. McIntyre, Norris, and Copenhaver (1981) have defined instructional planning as "the process by which teachers weigh alternative materials, methods, and means of evaluation in order to produce focused lessons." The proper use of instructional time cannot be "willed"; teachers must carefully plan how to achieve their instructional goals, making not only daily plans but long-range plans as well. Shavelson (1982) synthesized the research on teacher planning and reported on the five levels of planning identified by Yinger (1977).

1. *Long-range yearly*—basic ideas for social studies, science—some for math and reading—basic structure of what will be done but not specific time.
2. *Term*—planning on a term basis for social studies, science, and for movies.

3. *Monthly*—deciding on basic units for social studies, science, and math. I decide on what I need librarian to get or what movies I need.
4. *Weekly*—use teacher's plan book—specific units and time element added —more detailed.
5. *Daily*—put schedule on board, getting actual materials out. (p. 172)

Studies on teacher planning have indicated that recently teachers focus on instructional activities when making planning decisions (Zahorik, 1975; Clark & Yinger, 1979; Yinger, 1978). This focus on activities as the basic unit of planning applies not only to daily plans but to weekly and unit planning as well. Shavelson (1982) described the activity in a lesson as "the allocation of time, the sequencing and the timing (or pacing or flow) of content and materials during the lesson" (p. 26). This finding is in sharp contrast to traditional thinking, which says that teachers first focus on specific objectives in making planning decisions. However, this focus on activities should not be interpreted to mean one should not attend to objectives in the planning process. On the contrary, student strengths and weaknesses and specific objectives should be a part of your activities; they should help to shape and guide your activities into meaningful learning experiences.

Teaching a Lesson

The basic element of teaching is the individual lesson. Upon this foundation, teachers can design a series of lessons to attain instructional goals. The components of the lesson will be based on our knowledge of the students' readiness for learning and the knowledge we have accumulated about how to learn a new skill or ability. A basic component of teaching is the ability to show students how to do something new. A plan for teaching a lesson is given below, with a brief explanation of each component. The suggested elements of each component are just that—suggestions. Depending on the particular grade, students, and instructional goals, you can expect to modify the components to fit your situation.

Components in Teaching a Lesson
1. Major activity
2. Instructional goal
3. Materials
4. Motivation and background (readiness)
5. Teaching
6. Supervised practice
7. Independent practice
8. Evaluation

Major Activity

To help create a proper mind-set for teaching a new skill or ability, it is recommended that you first briefly list the major activity. Listed below are some examples:

Writing a character sketch
Auditory discrimination of vowel sounds
Use of the newspaper
Estimating with multiples of 10
Writing editorials
Short stories
Comparing fractional numbers
Punctuation marks
Exponential and logarithmic functions
Directed reading activity (using a basal reader)
Declension of irregular adjectives
Improvement of study skills
Summarizing *The Merchant of Venice*

Instructional Goal

Using the major activity you have chosen, you should state the goal of the lesson. This statement should explain exactly what you expect students to know or be able to do as a result of the lesson. If the lesson has a direct learning objective, the goal should be pinpointed with specificity, with the goal specified in terms of observable student behavior and a specified competency level. If the lesson has an inquiry objective, less specificity is required and the intended goal should reflect diagnostic information on students. Regardless of the grade and subject area, you should be teaching what the students need to know. This can be accomplished only by knowing the instructional needs of your students. Also, implicit in stating the instructional goal is your awareness of the prerequisite skills and knowledge that the students must possess to be successful in the lesson. Getting in the habit of identifying prerequisite skills and knowledge will greatly enhance student learning. You will be confident in evaluating student learning in a particular lesson, knowing students do not lack the prerequisite skills and knowledge.

Materials to Be Used

Listing the materials to be used in the lesson is an absolute necessity for teachers-in-training. While this component may seem mundane, it is important. The materials you select should be on the proper level of difficulty to help ensure student involvement. Knowing what materials you will be using and having them prepared before the class begins is a problem for some teachers-in-training. As you can anticipate, if materials are not ready to use, you may lose some or all control of the class. Management problems can follow; worst of all, you may be unable to realize the instructional goal.

Motivation and Background

This component highlights the beginning of your lesson. By motivating students, I mean attempting to enlist their interest in the topic of the lesson; developing background for the lesson entails reviewing past learnings related to the new information and concepts to be presented in the lesson, to help make the lesson relevant to students. There are numerous ways to motivate and to provide background for lessons, and below are some ideas that may prove useful:

Use illustrations in the text to develop interest.

Have students discuss a personal experience related to the major activity of the lesson.

Use direct experiences. Bring in real objects, make trips outside the class, invite in a guest lecturer, perform an experiment.

Discuss new concepts to avoid misconceptions.

Use the arts. Listen to music or display pieces of art.

By motivating and developing background you will be helping students create a mind-set for the material to follow. Time spent in this readiness phase will help students "tune in" to the lesson and help maintain their attention and concentration. This part of the lesson provides students with a purpose for learning. This purpose should be specific and it should relate to subsequent learning. Making sure students know the purpose of the lesson also helps keep their attention and improve their understanding.

Teaching

The heart of the lesson is teaching—the manner in which you explain, inform, show, or demonstrate what you want students to know. This can be done inductively, that is, with a step-by-step explanation, proceeding from the simple to the complex, and using examples and illustrations that lead students to a generalization. Or it may be done deductively, first telling students the generalization and then supplying examples to verify it. Where possible, concrete examples should be used to break down the new material into meaningful units. You should carefully plan classroom questions on an appropriate level of difficulty and at different levels of intellectual thought to determine student understanding and clarify difficult points. Also, you should allow sufficient time after posing a question before you respond to a student. Students need time (at least three seconds) to process the question and formulate an answer. Your sensitivity to "wait-time" (Rowe, 1974) will help increase classroom interaction and student learning. In addition, to check on student understanding and maintain student attention you should give specific verbal feedback with task-related comments and probing questions (see the Planning for Classroom Discussion section below for further explanation). You should always be ready to modify teaching procedures and materials based on the students' responses. If the students are encountering little difficulty, you should increase the pace of the lesson so that you do not lose them. If students are encountering difficulty, you may have to slow down and reteach the instructional goal in another fashion. Providing occasional restatements and summarizing main ideas are ways to develop and reaffirm intended goals. It is important for you to discover the degree to which the students are catching on and to give them the necessary feedback so that they know what needs improvement.

Supervised Practice

Before allowing students to complete an independent assignment it is important that you "walk" students through a few examples or through part of an independent activity and summarize key points. This will let you know if the students have understood your initial explanation and have begun to transfer this learning to a new situation.

Independent Practice

Meaningful practice should be provided to ensure transfer of a new skill or ability to a variety of situations. It is important to make sure that independent assignments are understandable to students. Depending on the instructional goal, you should still monitor such practice indirectly. In the case of direct instruction, even independent practice should be monitored, because more teacher involvement will mean more student learning. The independent practice should be on an appropriate level of difficulty to ensure a high success rate, and the practice should be plentiful enough for mastery and transfer of the new skill. Without practice to the point of overlearning and automaticity (application of the skill without thinking about it), students are likely to accumulate "half-learnings." In the case of inquiry instruction, teacher behavior is quite different. Instead of directing independent practice, you assume the role of a facilitator. There should be little concern for moving the practice along at a rapid pace, since the students should control the pacing of activities, the amount of interaction, and the instructional activities themselves. Regardless of the type of instructional goal, it is important that you recap the main points of the lesson at the end of the activity.

Evaluation

Evaluating a lesson to see if you achieved the prestated goal can be accomplished in a number of ways, for example, by using a worksheet, test, discussion, teacher-made or commercial game, or group activity. Evaluation is a process that should pervade each instructional lesson. Your monitoring and evaluating of student progress should be included in each part of your lesson. By doing so, student time-on-task will be increased throughout the lesson and final student achievement of the instructional goal will be realized. Whatever materials are used to evaluate whether the lesson's goal was achieved, you should check to make sure the evaluation reflects the instructional goal and content of the lesson. Other important points to consider in evaluating your lesson's objective are given in the Self-Monitoring FYI on Before and After: Important Considerations in Teaching a Lesson on page 68 and the FYI on Teacher-Made Tests on page 104. If students perform well, you can feel reasonably sure that your teaching was appropriate and your students are ready for the next step. If students did not achieve the objective of the lesson, it is necessary for you to re-examine your teaching procedures and decide how to reteach the original learning objective. This final lesson evaluation is the best feedback for both you and the students because it lets you know how to teach tomorrow's lesson.

Review of Key Lesson Components
- Major activity
- Instructional goal
- Materials
  - Be sure materials are ready at the start of the lesson.
- Motivation and background
  - Review past learnings.
  - Elicit student interest.
  - Communicate purpose of lesson.
- Teaching
  - Begin lesson with students on-task.
  - Present lesson inductively or deductively with many examples and illustrations.
  - Be sure the level of difficulty of the presentation is appropriate so that students will be successful.
  - Maintain a brisk pace.
  - Give feedback with task-related comments and probing questions.
  - Be sensitive to "wait-time."
  - Provide summary of main points.
- Supervised practice
  - Complete a few examples with students.
  - Provide appropriate feedback.
  - Summarize key points.

- Independent Practice
  - Make sure independent assignments are clear.
  - Make sure practice material is at an appropriate level of difficulty to ensure a high success rate.
  - Plan sufficient time and materials to achieve automaticity.
  - Monitor student practice by circulating around the room.
  - Recap main points.
- Evaluation

Unit Plans

As a college student, you do not take just one or two courses each semester but usually five or six. For this, you must be mentally prepared and must plan your semester schedule for attending class, doing homework, and allocating time for relaxation. As a teacher, instead of just teaching one subject for one or two class periods, you will teach a number of subjects and skills over several weeks and you must mentally prepare a teaching plan covering several days. Depending on the subject and the level you teach, the curriculum may already be divided into meaningful units around a particular theme. As a teacher-in-training, once you have had experience teaching an individual lesson, you may be required to teach either a mini-unit (four or five sequential lessons) or a long-range unit (nine or ten sequential lessons). The core of this set of plans remains the same—the individual lesson plan. The factors to keep in mind in planning a one or two week unit are the same for planning your semester or year activities. Although you will probably have curriculum guides to help in decision making, the following factors should be considered:

1. What are the major activities to be used as vehicles to teach instructional goals?
2. What are your general and specific instructional goals?
3. How much time are you tentatively allotting for each major activity?
4. How will you divide the material to be covered in reasonable units and proper sequence for instruction?
5. What is the prerequisite knowledge needed by the students to be successful in the unit?
6. How might other content subjects be integrated into the units?
7. What ways can you use to help the slow starter and motivate the fast starter who soon gets bogged down?

A suggested outline for a one week mini-unit and a two week long-range unit are given below.

One Week Mini-Unit
- Overall instructional goals
- Four or five sequential lessons
- Evaluation

Two Week Long-Range Unit
- Overall instructional goals (balance of direct and inquiry learnings)
- Specific questions students will be able to answer following instruction
- Individual lesson plans
- Unit evaluation
- Integration of other content areas
- Listing of books, films, records, computer software, magazines, and other supplemental materials appropriate to meet the goals of the unit

Flexible Lesson Planning

Although planning is absolutely crucial to successful teaching, too detailed a plan or too much reliance on the plan can thwart student learning. Certainly, you want to be prepared, but you must realize that students will not perform as expected 100 percent of the time. The "unexpected" or "unplanned" happens daily, and you must be able to respond properly. A few possible reasons that would warrant a change in your initial teaching plan are presented below:

Students exhibit greater understanding of the lesson goal than previously expected (or the reverse)

A student responds to a question with a creative or imaginative answer that in turn leads other students to relate similar concerns

Due to a class interruption, there is not enough class time left to finish the lesson.

In such situations, you must be sensitive to students' needs and modify your lesson accordingly. Rigidly following the lesson plan with a lack of sensitivity for the needs of the students defeats the purpose of lesson planning. Lesson planning is envisioning a blueprint for the achievement of your instructional goals, and you should include a measure of flexibility in a well-conceived plan. Remember, it is one thing to write a lesson plan two or three days before the day you will teach it, but it is quite another to execute the lesson creatively with students in the classroom. Many times your best lessons will not be entirely planned, if you are ready to respond depending on the needs of students.

Planning for Classroom Discussion

Since the core of a lesson is the "teaching" step, in which you explain, demonstrate, and discuss new learnings with your students, it is imperative that you carefully plan class discussion. The teacher's art of questioning is one important key to lively classroom discussions and how much students learn. Your ability to ask appropriate questions will affect student motivation and participation, development of comprehension skills in the subject area, and cognitive level of class discussions. Likewise, the students' responses can reveal their attitude and interest in learning and their achievement or lack of achievement of instructional goals.

Most teachers in training have been exposed to Bloom's *Taxonomy of Educational Objectives* (Bloom et al., 1956). Low-level questions are usually designated as those that represent Bloom's Knowledge and Comprehension categories and some of the Application category. High-level questions usually correspond to some questions in the Application category and questions in the Analysis, Synthesis, and Evaluation categories. Essentially, low-level questions range from dealing with concrete facts (the questions who, what, where, and when) to interpreting explicitly stated information (inferential questions, sometimes represented as how and why questions). High-level questions raise the level of thinking to creative and critical applications of information. Such questions stimulate abstract thinking (questions such as "what if" or "so what—what does it mean to me?").

Another way of categorizing classroom questions is to ask whether they encourage convergent or divergent thinking. Convergent thinking corresponds to low-level questions; these are questions that have a "right" answer. On the other hand, divergent thinking corresponds to high-level questions; these questions do not have a "right" answer. A sample question for each type of thinking is given below:

Convergent thinking: What was the name of the hotel manager?
Divergent thinking: Why do you think the author ended the story in this way?

As you can see, the convergent question has a right answer that can be verified. The divergent question may be answered in a number of ways, and each answer would be correct.

The type of questions asked depends on the instructional goals. In general, you should strive for a balance of low-level and high-level questions. This should be the goal, even though standardized and criterion-referenced tests mostly assess convergent thinking. Since the ultimate goal is to cultivate the students' ability to think independently, providing students with an opportunity to respond to a balanced pattern of discussion questions will stimulate their thinking on all levels.

When teaching a specific skill amenable to direct instruction, you should initially plan on asking a high percentage of low-level questions. After the students have mastered the skill on a factual level, they can be asked to use this new skill in answering high-level questions. Thus, reaching the low-level objectives will give students something to think with at a higher level. If you are developing a high-level thinking ability, you should concentrate on asking "thinking" questions, which will encourage students to rearrange the factual information they have learned in abstract and creative ways.

When you are conducting a discussion with students, situations will develop in which the students must be redirected or put back on the right track. They may need a question rephrased or further elaboration, or may need to be challenged to think critically. In such cases, it is helpful to give feedback with task-related comments and probing questions. As described in Chapter Three, task-related comments are statements to students that are specific to the work at hand. These comments are not of a general nature and help focus students' thinking on the intended goal and maintain classroom control. An example would be, "Tim, your answer to the first question is correct. Now, we will all complete the next five questions by ourselves and then we will go over the answers together." Probing questions are used to redirect and refine students' response to a question. The following are examples of probing questions:

Are you sure you mean what you said?
Can you give me another example?
What are some other alternatives?
Can you tell me more?
What assumptions are you making?
Can you explain why?
Do you agree? Disagree?

You could plan an excellent, balanced set of questions for discussion, but if you do not involve as many students as possible, the lesson will come up short. There are several methods of calling on students during class discussions. Since the literature on teaching has not conclusively shown one method to be more effective than others, it is recommended that you vary methods depending on the content, goals, and students. To find the method that works best for you and your students is the ultimate goal. Listed below are different methods of calling on students.

Decide which student to call on before asking a question.
Ask a question and call on a student who "wants" to answer it.
Ask a question and call on a student at random to answer it.
Phrase your question by first stating the student you want to answer the question.

To achieve the overall goal of maximizing student participation, you need to be accepting of student responses and show them (both verbally, with pleasant tone of voice, and without insulting them if they answer incorrectly, and nonverbally, through facial expressions) that you respect them and their ideas. You want to communicate a nonthreatening atmosphere in which they will feel free to respond and ask questions.

SELF-MONITORING FYI

Suggestions for Planning Discussion

1. Write discussion questions on 3 × 5 cards until you feel adroit in this area. As you may have already discovered, it is difficult to create specific questions extemporaneously during discussion.
2. Be certain your questions follow a logical pattern.
3. Make sure the questions are logical and are easy to understand. Be ready to reword a difficult question.
4. Plan how you intend to involve as many students as possible in the discussion.
5. Try to anticipate student responses.
6. Be sensitive to students' verbal and nonverbal responses to keep the pace running smoothly.
7. For feedback, use task-related comments that are directed specifically toward students' thinking.
8. Sustain the discussion around key ideas by using probing or clarifying questions.
9. Allow students adequate time to respond to questions (wait-time).
10. Monitor the types of questions you plan on asking and those asked by referring to the chart on Bloom's taxonomy.
11. Encourage students to ask questions.
12. Circulate around the room, never remaining in one place for an entire period.
13. Plan to have students summarize new knowledge.

SELF-MONITORING FYI

Before and After: Important Considerations in Teaching a Lesson

Before the Lesson:

What do you expect students to know and be able to do as a result of the lesson?

Can you improve upon the activities selected to achieve the instructional objectives?

What are you assuming students already know in order to achieve the goal you have chosen?

Are you thoroughly familiar with the activities and materials selected to accomplish the goal?

Is there a close match between the difficulty level of the activities and materials and the performance level of students?

Have you distinguished instructional goals from instructional activities?

How do you plan to explain to students how this lesson is related to a previous lesson or to future lessons?

After the Lesson:

Did you relate to students the importance of the goal of the lesson?

Did you circulate around the room to maintain student involvement?

Did you "read" the students to determine when "enough is enough"?

Did you finish the lesson on a positive note?

Did you plan enough varied and interesting practice to ensure transfer of the skill to other types of activities?

What checkup of mastery was made?

How was progress recorded?

Was the time too long or too short for the activity (or activities)?

What adaptations of your materials or procedures were made to meet the individual differences of students?

Did you have a concluding activity or wrap-up discussion?

Did students know what to do when they finished their independent assignment?

Did you distribute and collect materials at the right time?

Was there continuity in terms of information and motivation?

Did you stray too much from the topic at hand during class discussion?

How effective was the introduction to the lesson?

SELF-MONITORING FYI

Wait-Time

Definition: The amount of time a teacher waits after asking a question before making a response.

Tips:

- Research has shown that most teachers allow just one second after asking a question before making some type of response to a student.
- Students need three to five seconds to digest the question and formulate an answer.
- When adequate wait-time was allowed, the following changes occurred in classrooms:
  - The number of students who failed to respond when called on decreased.
  - The number of unsolicited but appropriate responses increased.

- The length of student responses increased.
- The number of student statements that used evidence to make inferences increased.
- The number of responses from students identified by the teacher as less able increased.
- The number of student-to-student interactions increased.
- The number of student questions increased (Rowe, 1974).
- Remember, "more is not necessarily better." Thirty seconds of wait-time is too much, and allowing it will stifle classroom interaction. Decisions about wait-time should depend on students' abilities and the content you are covering.

READER INTERACTION 4

Monitoring Instructional Functions
Using the chart below, examine your written daily lesson plans for one subject for a two week period. Each day, put a check mark next to each instructional function that you performed. For some lessons, you will be able to make more than one check mark and for others only one.

Synthesize and analyze the information from your chart by answering the following questions:

Which functions received the highest number of checks?

The lowest number of checks?

Do you feel an adequate balance was maintained among the six instructional functions for the content covered during the two week period?
yes   no
Explain

Do you disagree with any function and its applicability to your subject area?   yes   no
Why?

LESSON PLANS FOR TWO WEEKS

Instructional *Functions*	Day 1	Day 2	Day 3	Day 4	Day 5	Day 6	Day 7	Day 8	Day 9	Day 10
Daily Review and Checking Homework										
Presentation										
Guided Practice										
Correcting and Feedback										
Independent Practice (Seatwork)										
Weekly and Monthly Reviews										

READER INTERACTION 5

Lesson Evaluation Report

Ask another student teacher or your cooperating teacher to observe and complete a lesson evaluation on a lesson you teach. Record the absence or presence of each lesson component, and write as many comments as time allows. If one of the questions below is not appropriate to the lesson, write NA (not applicable) after the question. An alternative to monitoring a whole lesson would be to concentrate on one specific aspect of a lesson.

OBSERVATION REPORT

Lesson Objective: _____ Direct or Inquiry Learning? _____

Yes   No   *Comments*

_____ _____   *1. Motivation and Background:*
Was background information
given?
                                   _____

_____

_____ _____   Was the goal of the lesson
communicated to the
students?
                                   _____

_____

_____ _____   Was a purpose established
for completing the lesson?
                                   _____

_____

_____ _____   Were students motivated to
take an interest from the
beginning?
                                   _____

_____

_____ _____   *2. Teaching:*
Was the objective explained
adequately?
                                   _____

_____

_____ _____   Were sufficient examples and
illustrations given?
                                   _____

_____

_____ _____   Were the teaching materials
adapted to the students'
needs?
                                   _____

_____

_____ _____   Was a sufficient variety of
activities used?
                                   _____

_____

Yes   No

Comments

—— ——   Were occasional summaries
provided by the teacher?

—— ——   Was progress assessed and
rewarded?

—— ——   Were all students involved in
the lesson?

—— ——   Was the teacher sensitive to
wait-time?

—— ——   Were task-related comments
and probing questions used?

—— ——   3. *Supervised Practice:*
Did the teacher go over a
few examples with the
students?

—— ——   Was any reteaching
necessary?

—— ——   Did the teacher summarize
important points?

—— ——   4. *Independent Practice:*
Was the practice understood
by the students?

Yes   No   *Comments*

___ ___   Was enough time allocated
          for students to complete the
          practice?   _____

                                                           _____

___ ___   *Was there enough practice*
          for students to master the in-
          tended goal?   _____

                                                           _____

___ ___   *Did the teacher monitor the*
          practice?   _____

                                                           _____

___ ___   *Did the teacher recap main*
          points?   _____

                                                           _____

                    5. *Evaluation:*
___ ___   Did the teacher evaluate the
          intended goal?   _____

                                                           _____

___ ___   Did the students seem satis-
          fied with the lesson?   _____

                                                           _____

READER INTERACTION 6

Constructing Classroom Questions

Select a story or passage that you intend to use with students. Using Figure 4.3 as a guide, construct questions for the lesson. Be sure you have at least one question representing each category of Bloom's taxonomy.

Write your questions in the space below. After each question, identify the type of thinking it is intended to foster.

Monitoring Classroom Questions
Assess questioning skills by taping one of your lessons or by having another person observe the lesson. Using Figure 4.3 as a guide, rate the level of thinking required for each question asked and put a check mark under the appropriate cognitive level in Bloom's taxonomy. If it is not possible to tape the lesson, ask your cooperating teacher or a fellow teacher-in-training to evaluate and record the types of questions asked in a lesson.

After the lesson, tally the number of questions asked in each cognitive level. Next, respond to the following questions:

- Did you ask questions that made students think at various cognitive levels?

- What type of question did you ask the most?
  the least?
- Are you satisfied with the pattern of questions asked?   yes   no
  If you answered no, what will you do differently in subsequent lessons?

- Did you ask any probing questions to clarify a point or extend students' thinking?

QUESTIONING CATEGORY	BLOOM'S CATEGORY	STUDENT ACTIVITY	TYPICAL STEM WORDS
LOWER LEVEL	Knowledge	Remembering: Facts, Terms, Definitions, Concepts, Principles.	What?, List, Name, Define, Describe.
	Compre-hension	Understanding the meaning of material.	Explain, Interpret, Summarize, Give examples . . . , Predict, Translate.
	Application	Selecting a concept or	Compute, Solve,
HIGHER LEVEL		skill and using it to solve a problem.	Apply, Modify, Construct.
	Analysis	Breaking material down into its parts and explaining the hierarchical relations.	How does . . . apply? Why does . . . work? How does . . . relate to . . . ? What distinctions can be made about . . . and . . . ?
	Synthesis	Producing something orig-inal after having broken the material down into its component parts.	How do the data support . . . ? How would you design an experiment which investigates . . . ? What predictions can you make based upon the data?
	Evaluation	Making a judgment based upon a pre-established set of criteria.	What judgments can you make about . . . ? Compare and contrast . . . criteria for . . . ?

SELF-MONITORING CRITIQUE

1. In conducting class discussions, how do you know when to stop and go on to the next part of the lesson?

Do you wait for all students to indicate that they understand before moving on?

What are some possible solutions to this dilemma?

FIGURE 4.3 (at left) *Summary of Bloom's taxonomy and breakdown between lower- and higher-level questions (From* **Effective Classroom Questioning** *[p. 5] by Stephanie S. Goodwin, George W. Sharp, Edward F. Cloutier, Nancy A. Diamond, and Kathleen A. Dalgaard, n.d., Urbana-Champaign, IL: Course Development Division, Office of Instruction Resources, University of Illinois. Reproduction permitted. No copyright.)*

2. Can you think of an instructional goal that is conducive to the inductive method of explanation? An instructional goal that is conducive to the deductive method?

Which way do you prefer to explain new information to students?

3. Have you taught a lesson to a group of students and allowed independent practice to be completed on different levels of complexity according to student ability?

4. Have you taught a lesson on a higher-level thinking skill? Was the lesson successful? How different were your procedures?

Summary

This chapter synthesized findings and recommendations relating to the two major types of learnings: direct and inquiry. Direct learnings encompass knowledge of a subject that can be taught in a step-by-step fashion. Most standardized tests measure the mastery of direct learnings. The recommended approach to teach this body of knowledge is "direct instruction." In direct instruction, the teacher is in control of all aspects of the lesson content—pacing, practice, and so on. Students are taught a new skill or understanding through a very structured explanation and demonstration, teacher-supervised practice, and an independent practice cycle. Inquiry learnings, which are those learnings not amenable to behavioral objective statements, concern themselves with critical and creative abilities. Although students initially need to learn some critical thinking processes in a step-by-step manner, the recommended teaching strategy for inquiry learnings is characterized by less teacher structure and control and more student input and independence. However, both types of learnings are important and both types of teaching strategies should be included in a teacher's repertoire.

The research on and steps in the planning process were reviewed. Although the traditional thinking was focused first on learning objectives, research has indicated that teachers plan their lessons around activities. Included in the discussion of planning were elements of successful lessons, long-range unit considerations, necessity for flexibility, and important concerns in conducting the classroom discussion phase of teaching.

All of the principles of instruction discussed in this book are involved in delivering differentiated instruction. As you learn and practice other principles, you are encouraged to relate them to the instructional cycle covered in this chapter.

References

Bloom, B. S., Engelhart, M. D., Furst, E. J., Hill, W. H., & Krathwohl, D. R. (Eds.), (1956), *Taxonomy of educational objectives: The classification of education goals, Handbook I: Cognitive domain.* New York: David McKay.

Clark, C. M., & Yinger, R. J. (1979). *Three studies of teacher planning.* (Research Series No. 55). East Lansing, MI: Michigan State University. (ERIC Document Reproduction Service No. ED 175-855)

McIntyre, D. J., Norris, W. R., & Copenhaver, R. W. (1981). A study of the planning and teacher skills of preservice elementary teachers. *Kappan, 63,* 65–66.

Raths, L. E., Wassermann, S., Jonas, A., & Rothstein, A. M. (1966). *Teaching for thinking: Theory and application.* Columbus, OH: Merrill.

Raths, L. E., Wassermann, S., Jonas, A., & Rothstein, A. M. (1986). *Teaching for thinking: Theory, strategies, and activities for the classroom.* New York: Teachers College.

Rosenshine, B., & Stevens, R. (1986). Teaching functions. In M. C. Wittrock (Ed.), *Handbook of research on teaching.* New York: Macmillan.

Rowe, M. (1974). Wait-time and rewards as instructional variables, their influence on language logic and fate control: Part 1. Wait-time. *Journal of Research in Science Teaching, 11,* 81–94.

Shavelson, R. (1982). *Review of research on teachers' pedagogical judgments, plans and decisions.* Los Angeles, CA: Rand Corporation and University of California.

Yinger, R. J. (1977). *A study of teacher planning: Description and theory development using ethnographic and information processing models.* Unpublished doctoral dissertation, Michigan State University.

Yinger, R. J. (1978). A study of teacher planning: Description and a model of preactive decision making (Research Series No. 18). East Lansing, MI: Michigan State University.

Zahorik, J. A. (1975). Teachers' planning models. *Educational Leadership, 33,* 134–139.

Principles of Instruction

- Cultivate student feelings and emotions.

- Maintain effective classroom control.

- Provide an appropriate balance between fostering direct learnings and inquiry abilities.

- **Maximize the use of classroom time to teach students what they need to know.**

- Diagnose student strengths and weaknesses and provide instruction based on student needs.

- Use a variety of materials to teach what the students need to know.

- Believe in your ability as a teacher to make a difference and convince students that they will learn.

CHAPTER 5

Quality Time

Dimensions of Time

Studies of effective teaching and effective schools have yielded two important findings regarding time: first, the amount of time that is allocated to instruction in a particular subject affects how much students learn, and second, the way that this allocated time is used by teachers directly relates to student achievement (Denham & Lieberman, 1980). These findings reflect the two sides of time.

Allocated time refers to the time given to cover material in a course of study. Coverage entails scheduling sufficient time for both teacher and student to cover targeted instructional goals. This aspect of time refers to quantity, that is, the amount of time designated to cover instructional material. School districts or state education agencies usually decide how much time is to be allocated for instruction in any one area. However, teachers must use this time for instructional purposes. Although teachers do not have much influence over the amount of time allocated for instruction from an administrative scheduling standpoint, they can abuse the allocated time by not using the full amount for a particular subject. The evidence that teachers differ in the amount of time that they allot for instruction was reported in the Beginning Teacher Evaluation Study (BTES) (Fisher et al., 1978). This highly influential study showed that teachers who allocated more time than average to teaching math and reading in the elementary school produced higher than average student achievement. Researchers found surprising differences in the amount of time allocated for instruction. For second grade math, the average allocated time was from 25 minutes to 60 minutes per day in different classes. In fifth grade reading, the researchers found allocated time averaged from 60 to 140 minutes per day. The BTES researchers discovered equally surprising differences in the amount of time allocated for specific skills within subject areas. For example, in one fifth grade reading class an average of 10 minutes daily was spent on instruction in reading comprehension, in contrast to another class with an average of 50 minutes per day spent on comprehension instruction.

Stallings and Mohlman (1981) provided more specific data about the use of allocated class time by secondary school teachers. The authors reported that effective teachers spend less than 15 percent of the time on classroom management and organization matters. They spent 50 percent or more on interactive instruction with students, and no more than 35 percent of the time on monitoring independent seatwork activities. Thus, for a 50-minute class, approximately 6 to 8 minutes was spent on management and organization matters, at least 25 minutes on instruction, and from 15 to 18 minutes on seatwork assignments. All these findings reinforce the conclusion that students will not learn if they are not given the opportunity to learn. "Opportunity to learn" is perhaps the most powerful variable that accounts for how well students learn in school.

The other side of time refers to *how* the allocated time is used by teachers in the classroom. How time is used can vary greatly from classroom to classroom depending on instructional goals and teaching skills. This aspect of time is often referred to as quality time, the time when students are actually attending to the work at hand. Fortunately, classroom teachers have direct control over this dimension of time. Other terms for quality time are "student time-on-task" or "academic engaged time." Research on teaching clearly shows that the more time students spend engaged in learning, the higher their achievement will be. You should not be surprised to realize that during many minutes of a class students will not be actively working or paying attention. The BTES researchers also found surprising differences in the average engagement rates across various classes. They observed some classes where students were engaged 50 percent of the time and others where the students' time-on-task or engagement rate was close to 90 percent.

Academic Learning Time

The BTES researchers went a step beyond examining just engagement rate and looked at student success rate. A student may be on task but committing error after error. Students who are on task but also completing exercises successfully at a high rate learn more than students who may be engaged but completing exercises at a lower success rate. This high rate was called academic learning time (ALT) by Fisher et al. (1979), who defined the term as "the amount of time a student spends engaged in an academic task he/she performs with high success" (p. 52). A high success rate is considered to be above 80 percent. Academic learning time consists of three factors, allocated time, student engagement, and student success rate, and all three factors have been shown to contribute to increased student achievement. Academic learning time occurs when a student is given the time or opportunity to learn, is actively engaged with the task at hand, and is experiencing success with the task. Classrooms with high rates of academic learning time produce higher achievement in the area of direct learnings in school subjects.

Obviously, academic learning time results from the interplay of several factors. When you review Rosenshine's instructional functions, you can see that the teacher must be directing and guiding the entire learning cycle—initial teaching, demonstration, discussion, and practice. The key to academic learning time is a high degree of interaction between the teacher and students.

Examining Time Allocation

Obviously, how time is used in the classroom is interrelated to and interdependent upon the implementation of all the other principles of instruction. The importance of time can be appreciated if one looks at the school curriculum in terms of

1. time emphasis for the three components in teaching a subject area —developmental, independent, and corrective;
2. time emphasis for direct and inquiry learnings within each subject area.

As stated in Chapter One, all school subjects contain three components: the developmental program, the independent or recreational program, and the corrective program. Briefly, the instructional program encompasses the teaching of all the direct and inquiry learnings needed to attain understanding and appreciation of a particular subject. The recreational program denotes the time students spend practicing the knowledge and skills taught to them in the developmental program. It is also the goal of the recreational program to foster a positive attitude toward the subject at hand and to expand students' interests. The corrective program of any subject area deals with additional instruction and practice opportunities for students who for some reason fail to understand adequately the skill or topic being studied. A key to the proper use of allocated time is to maintain a balance in each subject area between the three major components. Ignoring one component will lead to problems in another. For example, spending 100 percent of the allocated time in American history on factual content is unlikely to produce students who want to do extended reading in this subject. Time must be given to use this factual content in a variety of independent activities. Due to the need to prepare students for basic skill tests and accountability pressures, it is not uncommon to find teachers giving a disproportionate amount of time to direct skills in the developmental phase. This is a mistake. To produce independent learners, a balanced program in each subject is necessary. Effective teachers know the components of a complete program in their subject area and plan to use a portion of the allocated time in each phase. This does not mean that in each day evidence of the developmental, recreational, and corrective programs should be given. Obviously, some days you might devote all the time to one or two of the components. However, you should see evidence of each of the components when examining weekly or monthly teaching plans. The second area to consider relative to the question of time is the relative emphasis given to the two broad types of learnings, direct and inquiry, within the instructional program. Just as it is important to strike a balance between the three components of a subject area, it is equally imperative that a balance be maintained within each subject area between direct and inquiry instruction. In addition, you should consider the time requirements for various skills within each of the two broad types of learning. Allocating sufficient time will depend on a host of factors, especially the complexity of the task and the characteristics of the students. Therefore, it is important to monitor instruction to ensure that you have allocated sufficient time for your students to learn.

One characteristic of effective teachers at every grade level is having a correct relationship to the two broad areas of learning (direct and inquiry), and this correct relationship is reflected in allocating sufficient time for both types of learning and using that time properly. Essentially, the different learnings require different teaching strategies, and these are ultimately reflected in the way time is used. Time for direct learnings is controlled and monitored very closely by the teacher, and all teacher-student interactions are judged with time-on-task as the primary factor. Time is important to the development of inquiry learnings as well, but how that time is used is quite different. Whereas a high degree of quickly paced teacher-student interaction is considered crucial in direct instruction, in inquiry learning the key element is allowing students ample time in a variety of activities to develop higher-level thinking abilities. Productive time is certainly of concern, but not in the traditional sense of quickly paced instruction with the teacher in command most of the time. For the development of inquiry goals, teachers assume the role of facilitator, not director. The teacher should indirectly monitor student involvement but most importantly allow time for student thinking and discovery. This time should include greater student participation and involvement in the application of ideas. Much more time needs to be allotted for independent activities in inquiry learnings than in direct learnings. In addition, there is also a distinction between goals of instruction and subsequent means of accomplishment in the two types of learning. In direct learning, application of a skill usually takes the form of a worksheet or game. In these cases there is a one-to-one correspondence between the goals of the lesson and the ensuing vehicle to practice the skill. In fostering inquiry learnings, it is most likely that a one-to-one correspondence between the goal and the activity will not be achieved. For example, if you want students to learn a problem-solving strategy, it is likely students will work on various projects to demonstrate mastery rather than completing a worksheet. How much time is allocated to meet instructional goals and how that time is used are decisions teachers have control over. Effective teachers assist students in becoming critical and creative learners. This means time is allocated and the use of that time is geared for developing thinking skills. In discussing this very point, Wassermann (1987) further stresses the importance of following through on a commitment to cultivate thinking in teaching:

> We must ask ourselves some hard questions. Do we really want students to think? Do we want them to become more critical and more questioning and less likely to accept things at face value? Do we want more critical debate in the

classroom and less reliance on the teacher as the authority? In our hearts we may believe that we are in favor of thinking, but in our practice we tend to reward those students who sit quietly and don't ask the kinds of questions that make us uncomfortable, who give us the answers we want and accept what we say as truth, who do as they are told. To keep the classroom running smoothly, we demand conformity and avoid controversy. We choose solutions, not healthy skepticism. Unfortunately, we cannot have it both ways. We cannot have a thinking classroom without the mess that is an adjunct of any productive and creative act. (p. 465)

Teachers who are convinced that inquiry learnings are worthwhile plan for students to be involved in various activities. Criteria which may be used to foster inquiry learnings are offered by Raths (1971). These criteria provide suggestions for modifying classroom activities to teach important learnings not given to specific behavioral objectives. As you design lessons on inquiry abilities, you are invited to employ one or more of these suggestions to make the learning more effective.

Criteria for Worthwhile Activities*
1. All other things being equal, one activity is more worthwhile than another if it permits children to make informed choices in carrying out the activity and to reflect on the consequences of their choices.
2. All other things being equal, one activity is more worthwhile than another if it assigns to students active roles in the learning situation rather than passive ones.
3. All other things being equal, one activity is more worthwhile than another if it asks students to engage in inquiry into ideas, applications of intellectual processes, or current problems, either personal or social.
4. All other things being equal, one activity is more worthwhile than another if it involves children with realia.
5. All other things being equal, one activity is more worthwhile than another if completion of the activity may be accomplished successfully by children at several different levels of ability.
6. All other things being equal, one activity is more worthwhile than another if it asks students to examine in a new setting an idea, an application of an intellectual process, or a current problem which has been previously studied.
7. All other things being equal, one activity is more worthwhile than another if it requires students to examine topics or issues that citizens in our society do not normally examine—and that are typically ignored by the major communication media in the nation.
8. All other things being equal, one activity is more worthwhile than

* From "Teaching without Specific Objectives" by J. Raths, 1971, *Educational Leadership, 28,* pp. 714–720. Copyright 1971 by the Association for Supervision and Curriculum Development. Reprinted by permission.

another if it involves students and faculty members in "risk" taking —not a risk of life or limb, but a risk of success or failure.

9. All other things being equal, one activity is more worthwhile than another if it requires students to rewrite, rehearse, and polish their initial efforts.

10. All other things being equal, one activity is more worthwhile than another if it involves students in the application and mastery of meaningful rules, standards, or disciplines.

11. All other things being equal, one activity is more worthwhile than another if it gives students a chance to share the planning, the carrying out of a plan, or the results of an activity with others.

12. All other things being equal, one activity is more worthwhile than another if it is relevant to the expressed purposes of the students.

Independent Seatwork

An often overlooked but crucial area with respect to academic learning time is the time students spend working on activities on their own. In some classes, students spend 50 to 70 percent of the time completing seatwork assignments (Rosenshine, 1979). It is much easier to keep students actively working when the teacher is formally directing the learning. It is quite a different matter to be certain students are actively engaged when completing independent activities. Responding to this challenge in a positive manner separates the effective teachers from those who do a minimal job.

The purpose of independent activities in direct instruction is to provide varied and meaningful practice to ensure mastery and transfer of the targeted skill. Without practice to the point of overlearning and automaticity (application of the skill without thinking about it), students are likely to accumulate "half-learnings." The best explanation or demonstration by a teacher is useless unless students can apply the skill. But the rub comes here—how can you maintain a high level of involvement during independent activities? There are three overriding considerations:

1. To prepare the students to complete independent activities by giving clear instructions, by going over the first few examples together, and by letting students know what to do if they have a question while completing the activity.

2. To monitor students' involvement during independent activities.

3. To make sure the independent activities are at a readability or difficulty level that permits students to experience a high level of success. If students experience unusual difficulty with independent activities, chances are great that time-on-task will be relatively low and instructional goals will not be achieved. A high level of success is usually associated with

students completing successfully 80 percent or more of the independent practice items. Being able to gauge the readability level of material to be used for independent activities and to match this level to students' competency and interest levels will significantly affect their academic learning time.

On the other hand, the provision of independent seatwork for developing inquiry abilities is guided by different purposes. Since your goals are not automaticity and a high percentage of time-on-task but providing varied and interesting opportunities for students to develop their thinking skills, your mode of operation is different. Therefore, you are encouraged first to ensure sufficient time for independent seatwork and second to encourage students to practice the targeted inquiry ability in ways that they choose. To attain higher-level cognitive tasks, you should allow the students more control over how the skill is to be developed and you should also allow them more movement and flexibility (Soar & Soar, 1983). It is important to remember that these conditions are the opposite for the development of direct learnings. This is not to say that you do not monitor the independent practice of inquiry abilities, but your monitoring should be less obtrusive.

Differential Emphasis: Control of Instructional Activities and Learning Outcomes

As you spend time in various classrooms, inevitably you will observe a teacher in total control of the instructional activity at one time, imposing less control at other times, and engaging in little direct control of the learning task at still other times. Control in this sense means deciding what is being taught and how it is presented, practiced, and evaluated (as opposed to control of behavior and freedom of movement in the class). You might ask if this apparently fickle classroom behavior is desirable or if it is indicative of poor planning, resulting in wasted time. Such a pattern of teacher behavior is desirable and should become part of your repertoire. The underlying reason for this recommendation is that different degrees of teacher control of learning activities are necessary for achieving different instructional goals (Soar & Soar, 1983). Using one style of control for all types of instruction is not conducive to all types of learning. Studies on teacher effectiveness have indicated that just as you need to allocate sufficient time for students to learn different instructional goals, you also need to develop a sensitivity to varying control of the learning activity in relation to the cognitive level of the task at hand. Soar and Soar summarized this relationship well:

> For simple, low-cognitive-level outcomes, greater teacher control was best; but for more complex learning, less control was best. If the lesson was a rote one of memorizing the multiplication table or a list of spelling words, a closely

structured drill would be appropriate. However, if pupils were solving complex problems or engaged in creative production, a much lower degree of control would be appropriate. (p. 73)

The researchers point out that a teacher can go overboard and be too controlling in terms of the learning activity. Based on their investigations, they recommend a middle-of-the-road philosophy, that is, an intermediate amount of teacher control, for greatest achievement gain. As we saw in Chapter Four and the discussion of direct and inquiry learnings, more control is generally needed for direct learnings and less for developing inquiry learnings. This ability to shift one's control of the learning activity depending upon the type of instructional outcome will not be developed overnight, of course. As with the important yet painstaking skill of finding the correct pace for each lesson, it is safe to predict that acquiring this skill will take practice, trial and error, and more practice. If you are aware of this aspect of time management and monitor your growth in this area, however, you will continue to refine this skill.

SELF-MONITORING FYI

Time-on-Task
Definition: The amount of allocated time a student is actively working at the task at hand.

Tips:
- Be involved. That is the key to time-on-task. Students have to be involved with the teacher or the material, preferably the former. The more the teacher directs and guides, the better.
- Be sensitive to the pace of your lesson. Maintain a rapid pace but slow down or speed up when necessary.
- Provide academic focused feedback during the teaching, supervised practice, and independent practice steps of direct instruction—the sooner, the better.
- Monitor independent seatwork. Be available to help students.
- Check to make sure students experience a high level of success with independent seatwork.
- Be certain your explanation of the skill and what you expect your students to accomplish are clear.
- Communicate to students what they are to do if they have a question while completing an independent assignment and what they are to do if they finish before the period is over.
- Be mindful of classroom management techniques from Chapter Three (physical proximity, task-related comments, and so forth).

SELF-MONITORING FYI

Some Ideas for Recreational Activities, Kindergarten–Grade 3
Reading a favorite book
Reading aloud to children
Making book jackets, bookmarks, streamers, mobiles, and posters
Doing creative writing assignments
Putting on or watching a puppet show
Constructing a mural or diorama
Writing and drawing a rebus story
Doing choral reading
Playing games
CAI (computer assisted instruction)—word processing or simulation programs
Dramatizing a poem or a story
Collecting and organizing information on a topic

Some Ideas for Recreational Activities, Grade 4–12
Reading aloud to students
Holding a debate
Playing games
Reading an article related to a recent lesson or unit study
Dramatizing a scene from a book
Using CAI—word processing or simulation programs
Collecting and organizing information on a topic
Writing a summary of a topic researched in the library
Conducting science experiments
Doing creative writing assignments
Reading the newspaper leisurely or with a specific task (for example, analyzing the
    views of a politician)
Constructing time-lines, graphs, maps, and charts

READER INTERACTION 7

Study of Student Time-on-Task
Directions:
1. Fill in the names of the students in your classroom on the seating chart.
2. While sitting in the back of the room, record the type of activity to be
    pursued and the beginning time. Next, observe each student for two to three
    seconds in a predetermined order. Record a check (✔) on the seating chart if
    the student is off-task (not listening attentively, exhibiting inappropriate
    overt behavior, or simply not doing what he or she is supposed to be doing,
    i.e., not working productively). If a student is paying attention and working

productively, do not place a mark of any kind in his or her block. Be sure to record the ending time for each instructional activity.
3. Repeat step 2 every ten minutes until the end of the period.
4. After the class period, tally the number of students who were off-task during each 10-minute cycle. Next total the number of students reviewed during each 10-minute cycle. Divide the total number of students off-task by the total number of students reviewed. The answer will yield the percentage of students off-task. Subtracting this number from 100 will yield the percentage of students on-task during the observation.

Example: Observer makes three reviews of a class during a 50-minute period. There are twenty-five students in the class (total of 75 students reviewed during the three cycles). During the three cycles, a total of eight students were off-task. You can differentiate each cycle on the seating chart by marking 1 - ✔ , 2 - ✔ , or 3 - ✔ for students off-task.
By dividing 8 by 75 we obtain

$$\frac{.106 = .11}{75 \,|\, 8.00}$$
$$\underline{75}$$
$$500$$
$$\underline{450}$$
$$50$$

This tells us that 11 percent of the class was off-task. Subtracting this total from 100, we can say that 89 percent of the class was on-task during the observation.

Fill in the blanks below on your observation:
Number of students off-task: _____
Number of students observed: _____
Percentage of students off-task: _____
Percentage of students on-task: _____
Do you notice a pattern to the number of students off-task and a particular instructional activity?

What do you think of the results?

Do you feel that any significant factors affected the results? The maturity level of the students? Grade level? Subject being taught?

STUDENT TIME-ON-TASK OBSERVATION FORM

Subject or Class: _____   Date: _____

Time Period: _____

Instructional Activities   Beginning Time   Ending Time

_____   _____   _____

_____   _____   _____

_____   _____   _____

_____   _____   _____

_____   _____   _____

_____   _____   _____

SEATING CHART

READER INTERACTION 8

Observation of Seatwork Assignment
Directions: At the end of a teaching day, select a class in which you gave students an independent seatwork assignment and respond to the following questions to reflect on the effectiveness of the activity.

Number of students in class: _____

1. Did you provide directions to students?   yes   no
   How?

2. Did you explain the purpose of the assignment?   yes   no
3. Did you circulate around the room helping students in need?
   yes   no
4. Were students allowed to ask questions of you or of other students if help was needed?   yes   no
5. Did all students finish the assignment at approximately the same time?
   yes   no
6. What did students do if they finished the assignment early?

7. Were some students bored? Were some challenged? What verbal and nonverbal cues were emitted to indicate this?

8. Approximately what percentage of students were on-task? _____

   Of that approximate time-on-task percentage, what percentage of students were working with a moderate or high success rate (approximation of academic learning time, or ALT)?

SELF-MONITORING CRITIQUE

1. Review a lesson you recently taught. Does having students off-task always indicate the same thing?   yes   no
   If your response is no, what are the different possibilities?

2. In your grade level and in a subject of your choice, do you feel there is sufficient balance between time allocated to developmental learning (including both direct and inquiry learnings) and to recreational learning (independent activities, e.g., time for free reading, panel discussions, research projects, educational games)?   yes   no
Why do you feel this way?

Do you feel differently for other subjects?

3. Looking back over a full week of teaching, do you feel your control of different learning activities varied in relation to the type of intended outcome?

In retrospect, should you have exercised more control, or less?

Summary

This chapter summarized key findings relating to a teacher's most precious commodity —instructional time with students. Allocated time refers to the amount of time given to a particular subject. Academic engaged time, or time-on-task, refers to that portion of allocated time in which students work at the task at hand. Teachers have direct control over this aspect of time. The literature on teacher effectiveness has indicated that successful teachers characteristically have their students on-task for a large percentage of time. The BTES researchers extended this concept to include not only allocated time and time-on-task but also success rate (academic learning time or ALT). With time such an important yet limited commodity, it was recommended that you monitor how much time is allocated first to various components in your subject area (developmental, independent, and corrective) and second to the two major types of learning (direct and inquiry). In addition, since students spend large portions of classroom time completing independent assignments, specific attention needs to be given to making this time both productive and enjoyable for students.

References

Denham, C., & Lieberman, A. (Eds.). (1980). *Time to learn: A review of the Beginning Teacher Evaluation Study.* Sacramento, CA: California State Commission for Teacher Preparation and Licensing. (ERIC No. ED 192 454)

Fisher, C., Berliner, D. C., Filby, N. N., Marliave, R., Cahen, L. S., Dishaw, M. M., & Moore, J. E. (1978). *Teaching and learning in the elementary school: A summary of the Beginning Teacher Evaluation Study.* Washington, DC: National Institute of Education.

Fisher, C., Marliave, R., & Filby, N. (1979). Improving teaching by increasing academic learning time. *Educational Leadership, 37,* 52–54.

Raths, J. (1971). Teaching without specific objectives. *Educational Leadership, 28,* 714–720.

Rosenshine, B. (1979). Content, time and direct instruction. In P. Peterson and H. Walberg (Eds.), *Research on Teaching: Concepts, finds, and implications.* Berkeley, CA: McCutchan.

Soar, R. S., & Soar, R. M. (1983). Content effects in the teaching-learning process. In D. C. Smith (Ed.), *Essential knowledge for beginning educators* (65–75). Washington, DC: American Association of Colleges for Teacher Education. (ERIC No. SP 022 600)

Stallings, J., & Mohlman, G. (1981). *School policy, leadership style, teacher change and student behavior in eight schools,* Final report. Washington, DC: National Institute of Education.

Wassermann, S. (1987). Teaching for thinking: Louis E. Raths revisited. *Kappan, 68,* 460–465.

Principles of Instruction

- Cultivate student feelings and emotions.
- Maintain effective classroom control.
- Provide an appropriate balance between fostering direct learnings and inquiry abilities.
- Maximize the use of classroom time to teach students what they need to know.
- **Diagnose student strengths and weaknesses and provide instruction based on student needs.**
- Use a variety of materials to teach what the students need to know.
- Believe in your ability as a teacher to make a difference and convince students that they will learn.

CHAPTER 6

Diagnosis and Prescription

The Diagnostic-Prescriptive Process

Effective teachers at any grade level select and modify instructional goals in relation to what their students need; therefore, the decisions teachers make need to be based on diagnostic information gathered on their students. Research on teaching has reaffirmed the widely accepted belief in the importance of educational diagnosis (Fisher et al., 1980). As I emphasized earlier, research on teaching has yielded no simple recipe for teaching success, but it has revealed that because students, subject areas, and instructional goals are different, effective teaching methods will vary. Inherent in this statement is the necessity for diagnosis as a prerequisite for good teaching. Diagnosis is defined as a process whereby students' strengths and weaknesses in a given area are determined. Effective teaching is founded on a diagnostic framework. At the same time, the diagnostic process depends upon knowing the instructional goals in your subject and realizing students will be achieving at different levels with respect to those goals. The reasons for the latter are various, and include physical, emotional, psychological, social, cultural, mental, and educational factors. However, diagnosing students' needs by itself is not enough. Identifying student needs should lead directly to prescribing appropriate learning activities. The diagnostic-prescriptive process implies that you will determine where students are in relation to the instructional goals of your program and prescribe an instructional plan based on this diagnosis to help the students be successful and learn. The diagram on p. 98 depicts the steps in the diagnostic-prescriptive process.

Educational diagnosis is a process that permeates all instruction. However, at first glance, it may not be that evident. If you are observing a classroom, you may be overwhelmed watching the teacher "doing" a great many things. However, all this doing is based on much diagnostic thinking before, during, and after

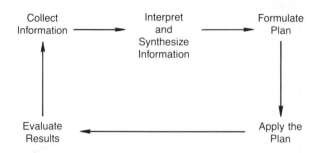

instruction. Effective teachers collect relevant information on students, interpret and synthesize this information, and plan and prescribe instruction according to student needs. They continually evaluate and reshape teaching decisions depending on a student's progress. Thus, the diagnostic process intrinsically affects the entire teaching-learning cycle. Underlying this process is a deep respect for the individual student. By seeking out diagnostic information on students to plan appropriate instruction, teachers are communicating a compassionate and respectful attitude toward the teaching-learning situation. To illustrate how diagnosis is an integral part of all facets of teaching, the following is a list of just some of the decisions or actions that depend on the diagnostic process:

Deciding on the content of lesson plans.
Determining the types of questions to ask students.
Determining the type of homework to be assigned.
Analyzing the essential components of an intended unit of study.
Developing teacher-made materials for instructional purposes.
Deciding on various informal and formal assessment techniques.
Deciding on the initial placement of a student in a class.
Deciding when to reteach a particular skill.
Designing tests at the end of a lesson or unit.
Reporting on a student's progress to parents.
Determining the content of class handout sheets.
Recommending students for special services.
Increasing student motivation for completing assigned activities.
Constructing teacher-made tests.
Pinpointing areas causing difficulty in a subject area.
Determining the effectiveness of a particular teaching strategy.
Determining how well instructional goals have been realized.

In relation to the two broad types of learnings—direct and inquiry—basing instruction on diagnostic information will help you to keep clearly in mind what you want students to learn. Being able to justify why you are doing what you are doing is one characteristic of an effective teacher. Guiding students in an inquiry ability, in such activities as classifying information into meaningful categories, requires you to assess students' entry abilities carefully and plan activities that will challenge them. Research on teaching direct learnings has supported the importance of diagnosis on increasing student time-on-task. As stated previously, one of the components of a high percentage of academic learning time is that students enjoy a high success rate (or low error rate). The probability for success is raised for a given task if students work on a "just right" level, that is, at their instructional level. Without initial and continual diagnosis of students' abilities, the likelihood of success and thus a high time-on-task percentage is not favorable. Working at one's frustration level (i.e., when the work is too difficult) all but eliminates the chance of producing significant achievement in direct learnings. Also, the crucial components of monitoring student progress and providing feedback in the direct instruction model are based on the teacher's accurately diagnosing and responding to student progress.

Types of Diagnostic Decisions

Being an effective diagnostician will enable you to match classroom instruction to instructional goals. Given the nature of individual differences, it is important to realize that different levels of diagnosis are required for students with different learning needs. The purpose of this discussion is to present the basic information on diagnosis that is required by classroom teachers. Students with special learning problems or severe disabilities will of course require the services of a trained clinician for a full diagnostic profile. Classroom teachers are expected to refer such students for further testing, but they are not responsible for diagnosing them.

Classroom teachers can be expected to diagnose their class at an analytical level at the beginning of the school year and to diagnose students' progress continuously throughout the school year. An analytical level of diagnosis requires teachers to make four types of decisions:

1. To determine the general achievement levels in the class
2. To identify individual differences within the class
3. To determine the needs of the class
4. To identify students in need of further diagnosis.

Standardized and Criterion-Referenced Tests

These four decisions can be made based on a combination of formal and informal measures and teacher observation. Formal measures include standardized achievement tests and commercially prepared criterion-referenced tests. Because you have probably studied educational assessment in other coursework, it is not the intention here to delve into this area in detail. However, for purposes of review, a brief comparison between standardized achievement and criterion-referenced tests is presented below.

Standardized Achievement Tests

Usually computerized, these tests interpret an individual's knowledge of a course of study on the basis of the performance of other students of the same age (norm group) on the same test.

Purpose: To measure what students have learned in a specific subject.

Reporting of results: These tests report student performances in a variety of forms including raw scores, percentiles, percentile bands, stanines, and grade equivalents.

Examples of standardized achievement tests:
    Comprehensive Test of Basic Skills (CTBS)
    Stanford Achievement Test
    Iowa Test of Basic Skills
    SRA Achievement Series
    Sequential Test of Educational Progress (STEP)

Criterion-Referenced Tests

These tests measure a student's performance with regard to an objective or criterion.

Purpose: To measure which student objectives have been achieved in a specific subject.

Reporting of results: Percentage of questions answered correctly for each specific objective and total number of objectives mastered.

Examples of criterion-referenced tests:
    Objective-Referenced Bank of Items and Test (ORBIT) (CTB/McGraw-Hill)
    State-mandated basic skill tests (minimum competency tests)
    Commercially prepared reading and math skill assessment programs
    Teacher-prepared tests to determine if students have reached a desired standard or criterion in a specific area.

Most achievement tests provide "ballpark" information on students, that is, on their general achievement levels. Thus, they are survey tests indicating overall achievement levels. However, some standardized tests furnish diagnostic information on students' performance, breaking down a subject area into component parts and providing separate subscores on each component in addition to an overall score. Standardized tests with this feature and criterion-referenced tests can provide more specific information on students. The more specific the information collected, the more valuable the test data will be in making diagnostic-prescriptive decisions.

Since new tests are continually being developed and old tests revised, it is difficult to remain current with all the standardized and criterion-referenced tests in your area. Two excellent sources of information about tests are the professional journals in your area (most include a test review section) and *Mental Measurement Yearbook*, edited by Buros (1984). This volume, updated annually, is probably the most authoritative source of information on published tests. It contains test reviews by recognized authorities in the field of assessment and is available in the reference section of most libraries.

Informal Measures

Informal measures include teacher-made tests, various checklists for particular behaviors, skill inventories, interest inventories, and daily assignments.

Placing a student in the proper level of instructional materials (i.e., at the instructional level) is an important step in ensuring successful learning. If students are trying to learn from materials that are too difficult for them (that is, at their frustration level), it is safe to predict that few will be as successful as they should be in learning. Matching the difficulty or readability level of class materials to your students' performance level should be one of your concerns throughout the year. One way to determine which students can be successful with a particular content textbook at the beginning of the year is to devise a teacher-made content area reading inventory (CARI) (Vacca & Vacca, 1986). This approach is applicable for content subjects from grades four through twelve. The authors suggest the inventory be used at the beginning of either a course or an instructional unit. They recommend that the inventory focus on assessing students' skills at locating information, comprehension abilities, vocabulary skills, and reading rate. Locational skills are assessed by first determining the particular skills (for example, the use of maps, diagrams, index, library materials) needed in the subject and then designing a series of questions for students to answer. Vocabulary abilities are assessed by preparing exercises that require students to show their competence in using contextual clues, their knowledge of word structure, and their dictionary skills. Determining students' strengths and weaknesses in the area of comprehension can be accomplished by selecting a passage from the text of 500 to 1,000 words and composing 10 to 15 comprehension questions for the students to answer. Students are to read the passage silently and answer the questions. These questions should assess the types of skills you deem important in your subject area and should span the different levels of comprehension (literal, interpretative, and critical). By counting the total number of words in the passage and providing each student with his or her silent reading time using a stopwatch, you will be able to determine both a percentage of comprehension questions answered correctly and a reading rate. Students answering at least 75 percent of the questions correctly will most likely be successful in reading and learning from that particular content textbook. To ascertain the proper beginning or placement level for elementary students in reading and math, it is recommended that you administer one of a variety of informal reading inventories or criterion-referenced pretests (see Heilman, Blair, and Rupley, 1986).

Advantages of teacher-made diagnostic tests over standardized tests include the ability to note more specific strengths and weaknesses, to more readily establish groups from information collected, and to more closely measure small increments of growth. By far, teacher-made tests are the best measures of general and specific achievement levels in class, of determining appropriate learning activities, and of ascertaining if your instructional goals have been achieved.

Thus, not only at the beginning of the year but throughout the year, teacher-made tests are best for ascertaining if students have achieved your objectives, because your own tests will mirror instruction far better than any standardized test. Teacher-made tests will provide valuable diagnostic information that should improve not only your students' learning but your teaching as well. Due to the nature of teacher-made tests, the amount of diagnostic information they will yield far outdistances standardized tests. Extreme care should be given in designing test items that accurately reflect your instruction. In addition, careful analysis of the test results vis-à-vis item difficulty and class response patterns can help in evaluating the results (Carlson, 1985).

Other forms of informal measures are daily assignment sheets and handouts for homework. Much diagnostic information can be gleaned from these sources besides total percentage of correct responses. As with teacher-made tests, item difficulty and individual and group response patterns can provide you with diagnostic information both to modify instruction and to improve future worksheets.

Teacher Observation

The most powerful diagnostic tool is keen teacher observation. If you really observe, knowing what to look for and what to listen for and then translating this information into instructional decisions will enable you to better match your teaching techniques to student needs. In this sense, observation becomes a teaching tool. In reality, it must be acknowledged that some teachers can spend all day with students but not really see or know them. To really observe you must be armed with the knowledge of essential learnings in your subject area, possess a basic understanding of the developmental characteristics of students, and focus your attention on a specific area.

Observation in three areas—of students, of the classroom, and of one's own teaching—can yield valuable diagnostic information. Observing students during instruction can help pinpoint their strengths and weaknesses. A teacher may informally observe and note student responses or use a structured observation scale. The overriding criterion is knowing precisely what you are observing.

Understanding the effect of the classroom environment itself on student learning is important to providing good instruction. The seating arrangements, use of classroom space, different grouping plans, and sound levels can be observed informally or in a more structured fashion. Many times a change in the physical environment will affect student learning, either positively or negatively.

Looking at one's own teaching is sometimes called diagnosis of instruction. Too often, we only look at students and never examine ourselves and our programs. Most of the Reader Interaction assignments within this text are aimed at diagnosis of instruction and at encouraging you to develop this habit of looking at yourself as well as at your students.

Observation is a powerful tool for classroom teachers when information from each of the three areas is combined with personal and background knowledge of your students. Determining a student's present level of performance and specific strengths and weaknesses is essential to providing appropriate instruction. However, since you will be grouping students for various purposes, it is also important to be able to survey the performance of an entire class and to determine achievement levels and common deficiency patterns. For this reason, it is helpful to design a class record sheet with specific information from various sources on each student. By profiling the abilities of the entire class, it facilitates making the four analytical diagnostic decisions.

The ability to translate these observations into meaningful classroom experiences would be weakened if you did not "know" your students. This "knowing" involves gathering background information (test scores, special learning characteristics) and learning personal characteristics (home background, family members, interests). Your ability to relate to your students, to motivate them to learn, and to select appropriate learning experiences will be based on this diagnostic process. As previously stressed, it is one matter to collect necessary information on students and the learning situation but quite another to use the information collected appropriately. The quality of classroom time is dependent on this diagnostic-prescriptive process, and the key to this process is collecting as specific information as possible and noting significant patterns of difficulty. The equation reads: More specific information collected equals better quality of instruction equals more student learning. For this reason, you are encouraged to gather as much information on students as possible from as many sources as possible. It is crucial to combine your observations with various test scores. In spite of the ever-increasing number and quality of tests on the market, tests are fallible. As yet, we simply do not have the degree of precision in tests that we would like to believe that we have.

Continuous Diagnosis

Realizing the achievement levels, individual differences, and needs in a class, teachers should design activities to match student needs. Also, teachers should be sensitive to identifying common difficulty patterns in their students throughout the year. In most classrooms, this means teachers will adjust their instructional approach to meet the changing needs of their students. After collecting data on students you must interpret the data and formulate prescriptive hunches or hypotheses. These hypotheses are then translated into appropriate learning activities. Each day's lesson becomes diagnostic material for tomorrow's lesson. This highlights the last essential of the diagnostic-prescriptive process —continuous diagnosis. Without it, instruction becomes stagnant and unproductive. The diagnostic teacher evaluates each day's lessons and makes adjustments in future lessons. If program modifications are not taking place, diagnostic teaching is not occurring.

SELF-MONITORING FYI

Functional Levels of Understanding

Independent Level: the "easy" level, in which the student can complete material with no support from the teacher.

Instructional Level: the "just right" level, in which the student can complete material with some support from the teacher (challenging but not too difficult).

Frustration Level: the "too difficult" level, in which the student cannot handle the material.

SELF-MONITORING FYI

Teacher-Made Tests

Points to consider:

- Check to make sure your test questions reflect the content and instructional goals of your course.
- Try to match your instructional goals with most appropriate type of items (essay or objective).
- Make sure your instructional emphases are reflected in the number of test items.
- Use a variety of objective questions in addition to multiple-choice (matching, completing, true-false, short answer, rank order, master list).
- Make sure the directions for the test are clear.
- Use the same language in writing test items as you used in class describing specific content.
- Make sure the test questions are written on an appropriate level of difficulty.
- After scoring the test, evaluate your students' responses.
  Ask yourself if the questions were too easy or too difficult.
  Notice if there was an item or two that every student missed.
  Ask your students if the test questions were fair and understandable.

Make adjustments to improve your next test.
Use test results to adjust future instruction.

SELF-MONITORING FYI

Record-keeping
Main Concept: Effective teachers maintain a record of their students' strengths and weaknesses in order to continuously teach students what they need to know.

Tips:
Keep records in a manner that fits your style. There is no "correct" way to keep records.

Maintain records on the absence or presence of the important learnings in your subject area. Note the frequency of their occurrence and adjust your instruction accordingly.

Involve your students in record-keeping and evaluation whenever possible.

Streamline your record-keeping procedures. Do not let them take up more time than necessary.

SELF-MONITORING FYI

Standardized Test Reporting
Standardized tests are norm-referenced; as such, the scores reported compare a student's performance with that of a representative group of students (norm group). The raw score on a test is the number of items answered correctly. Raw scores are then converted into norm-referenced scores. Scores are reported for each subtest, and a total achievement score is given.

Grade Equivalent: Expressed in grades and tenths of grades, this score indicates the grade level obtained by the average student in a norm group for a particular number of correct test items. For example, a grade equivalent of 5.8 means the student performed as well as the average student in the eighth month of the fifth grade in the norm group.

Percentile: A student score relative to the percentage of other students falling at or below that score. For example, a percentile rank of 55 means the student performed as well as or better than 55 percent of the norm population.

Stanine: A type of standard score with a mean of five and a standard deviation of approximately two. Stanines are scores that are distributed into nine parts and range from 1 through 9. Each stanine can be equated to an approximate percentage of scores in the norm group. Stanine 5 is the mean or average score.

READER INTERACTION 9

Teacher Interview

Rationale and directions: To gain an appreciation and a more thorough under-standing of the diagnostic process at your grade level, use the following ques-tions to interview your cooperating teacher or your grade level chairperson. Record your respondent's answers and later reflect on them.

Interview Questions

1. Do you use diagnostic and achievement tests?   yes   no
   Which ones?

   Are informal tests used?   yes   no
   What type?

2. What is the range of achievement in your class?

3. What are the overall strengths and weaknesses of your students?

How does this affect your instruction?

What modifications do you make?

Which students are in need of special assistance or instruction?

READER INTERACTION 10

Diagnosis and Prescription
Directions: Gather standardized and informal test data on one student in the classroom (remember to maintain the anonymity of the student). Use test data and other significant information to prescribe an instructional program for the student.

Diagnosis
Test Data (List test and results)

Insights from your observation of student

Student interests

Student strengths

Student Weaknesses

Preferred Learning Style

Prescription
Instructional Goals

Level of material appropriate for instruction

Special Materials and Activities

Motivational Strategies

Type of Adjustments To Ensure Success

SELF-MONITORING CRITIQUE

1. Millions of standardized tests are administered each year to students in schools across the country. How are the results of standardized tests used in your current situation? What decisions are made based on these tests?

2. Teacher observation is a powerful diagnostic tool. What are the specific student performance areas you would closely watch in your subject area? (If you are in an elementary grade, pick just one subject.)

3. There are limitations to every type of test. What are the limitations to criterion-referenced basic skills tests?

Summary

At the heart of effective instruction is the teacher's ability to diagnose students' needs. All facets of the teaching-learning cycle are dependent upon the process of diagnosis —especially the teacher's ability to use time effectively and efficiently, to maintain a high percentage of time-on-task, and to provide differentiated instruction. Classroom teachers at all levels are expected to diagnose their students at an analytical level. This diagnosis helps teachers make four types of decisions—about general achievement levels in their class, individual differences, needs of class, and students in need of further diagnosis. To achieve these results, teachers regularly collect information from tests (standardized, criterion-referenced, informal, and teacher-made) and teacher observation. After collecting various diagnostic information on students, teachers interpret the information and prescribe appropriate instruction. The effective teacher characteristically allows the diagnostic process to permeate all aspects of instruction—from making initial placement decisions to adjusting daily instruction based upon yesterday's lesson.

References

Buros, O. (Ed.). (1984). *The eighth mental measurement yearbook.* Highland Park, NJ: Gryphon Press.

Carlson, S. B. (1985). *10 designs for assessment and instruction.* Princeton, NJ: Educational Testing Service.

Fisher, C., Berliner, D., Filby, N., Marliave, R., Cahen, L., & Dishaw, M. (1980). Teaching behaviors, academic learning time, and student achievement: An overview. In C. Denham & A. Lieberman (Eds.), *Time to learn.* Washington, DC: National Institute of Education.

Heilman, A. W., Blair, T. R. & Rupley, W. H. (1986). *Principles and practices of teaching reading.* Columbus, OH: Merrill.

Vacca, R. T., & Vacca, J. L. (1986). *Content area reading* (2nd ed.). Boston: Little, Brown.

Principles of Instruction

- Cultivate student feelings and emotions.
- Maintain effective classroom control.
- Provide an appropriate balance between fostering direct learnings and inquiry abilities.
- Maximize the use of classroom time to teach students what they need to know.
- Diagnose student strengths and weaknesses and provide instruction based on student needs.
- **Use a variety of materials to teach what the students need to know.**
- Believe in your ability as a teacher to make a difference and convince students that they will learn.

CHAPTER 7

Variety of Materials

Types of Materials

To meet the needs of their students, effective teachers use a variety of instructional activities. As a part of these instructional activities, teachers select appropriate materials that are consistent with their diagnostic-prescriptive program, and thus these materials are vehicles to achieve one's instructional goals. Whether you are explaining a new skill, providing supervised or independent practice, or fostering recreational reading opportunities, you and your students will be interacting with some type of material. Making arrangements for your instruction (yearly, by semester, monthly, weekly, and daily) will require you to plan activities with at least ten main types of materials:

1. Main textbook(s)
2. Supplemental textbooks and enrichment books
3. Reference books
4. Paperback books
5. Newspapers, magazines, and various periodicals
6. Commercial learning kits
7. Workbooks and dittos
8. Realia: concrete objects, art work, math manipulatives, maps, charts, science experiments, diagrams, computers, tape recorders, VCRs, television, records; in addition, for kindergarten and primary grades (1–3), cut-out letters, pictures, picture dictionary, and Language Experience materials
9. Literature books
10. Teacher-made materials

Of course, many of the ten types of materials overlap in terms of how they may be utilized in the classroom. A more viable consolidation yields three major categories: main textbooks for your course(s) of study, supplemental materials, and teacher-made materials. Below, each main category is listed with its primary purpose(s) and the key concerns you should consider in selection and use:

Main Textbooks
Purpose: Primary vehicle(s) to cover content in a course of study.
Key Concerns:
    Is the readability level appropriate for students?
    Is the format conducive to learning?
    Is the sequence of presentation appropriate?
    Is the presentation clear?
    Is sufficient information presented to develop your content to acceptable
       levels of proficiency?

Supplemental Materials	*Teacher-Made Materials*
Purpose: To reinforce and extend previously taught skills and concepts.	Purpose: May be used as primary texts but more often are used to reinforce and extend previously taught skills and concepts.

Key Concerns
Do the materials reflect student interests and preferred mode of learning or both?
Do the materials represent a variety of readability levels to match student abilities?
Do the materials relate directly to your instructional goals (or do the materials reinforce and extend what students need to know)?
Are the materials applicable to the grouping plan you anticipate using (individual, small group, large group)?
Do the materials follow an acceptable sequence?
Do you need to supply feedback, or are the materials self-correcting in nature?

Computer Assisted Instruction (CAI)

The emergence of computers in our schools and classrooms has led to one indisputable fact: Opportunities for students to interact with a computer for instructional purposes are now available and will increase in each succeeding year (Shalaway, 1980). Computers are utilized for several purposes in our schools including diagnostic testing and reporting, computerized learning prescriptions, and instruction. However, since microcomputers did not become available in school classrooms until 1977, we still lack solid research to guide us in using CAI in the classroom (Schaudt, 1987). In spite of the relative newness of microcomputers, most schools have either computer labs or microcomputers in individual classrooms with software for most subjects.

As teachers-in-training, you will have several primary concerns:

1. In what ways can the computer be integrated into your instructional program to enhance student learning?
2. How effective is CAI in terms of student reaction and achievement in a particular subject area?
3. How effective is the software, and who decides which programs students will complete?

The first concern is addressed by examining your instructional goals and deciding how computers can assist in their development. You will need to try out ways of incorporating computers in your class and monitoring their effectiveness. The second concern can be assessed through both informal and formal tests. The third concern deals directly with the quality of computer software. Microcomputers should be treated like any other instructional material, and they should be viewed as vehicles to help you accomplish your instructional goals. Whether or not CAI will be a plus to students will mainly depend on the quality of the software and how that software is utilized. There are numerous software programs in every subject, and more are being developed all the time. There are four types of software programs: drill and practice, tutorial, simulation, and games. The majority of software programs for the classroom are in the form of drill and practice and are designed to practice and reinforce skills previously taught by teachers. In a typical sequence in this form of computer assisted instruction, a question is presented on the screen; the student responds; and the computer answers with "correct," "incorrect," or "let's try again." Many drill and practice programs provide teachers with a report card detailing the percentage of items answered correctly and significant error patterns. Tutorial software programs not only provide practice but carry on a dialogue with students by giving an explanation of a skill. The tutorial program is more complex than the drill and practice program, since there is more interaction between the computer and the student. When an incorrect response is made by the student, the tutorial program will indicate that the response is incorrect, explain why it is incorrect, reteach the skill, and give the student a similar item to attempt. Simulation software presents hypothetical situations that require students to respond. These programs have more inherent motivational value than either of the previously mentioned types and offer a unique method to develop thinking skills and problem-solving abilities. Learning games are a popular type of software programs that usually employs a drill and practice format to practice previously taught skills.

Quantity of software is not a major problem for teachers, but quality is. You must exercise your knowledge of the subject area and of the students to select appropriate software. One overriding recommendation is to always try the

	Good	Adequate	Poor
Type of Program			
___ drill and practice	___	___	___
___ tutorial	___	___	___
___ simulation	___	___	___
___ learning game	___	___	___
Ease of Use/User Friendly			
clear directions	___	___	___
exit capabilities	___	___	___
control of pacing	___	___	___
provision of help	___	___	___
Instructional Design			
objective made clear to student	___	___	___
introductory explanation of skill	___	___	___
sample exercises	___	___	___
number of practice exercises	___	___	___
immediate and varied feedback	___	___	___
branching capability	___	___	___
built-in assessment of progress	___	___	___
monitoring of student responses	___	___	___
corrections made by reteaching, giving clues, or explaining skill	___	___	___
summary statement	___	___	___
length of program	___	___	___
appropriate difficulty level	___	___	___
Content Accuracy			
direct correspondence between lesson objective and lesson procedures	___	___	___
accuracy	___	___	___
procedures reflect what a reader has to do in the process of reading	___	___	___
correct sequence used in presenting skill	___	___	___
Special Features			
animation	___	___	___
speech	___	___	___
music	___	___	___
laser videodiscs	___	___	___
touch screen	___	___	___
graphics	___	___	___
audio	___	___	___
color	___	___	___

software yourself before buying it and requiring students to spend instructional time with it. Figure 7.1 presents a software selection guide, examining the type of program, ease of use, instructional design, content accuracy, and special features. Computers are in the schools; however, you need to exercise control over how they are used in your subject area and which programs will be used with students.

Quantity-Quality Issue

Effective teachers use a greater variety of materials in their subject to engage their students to learn than less effective teachers do. In reality, the use of a variety of materials is intertwined with each principle of instruction—student affect, classroom management and organization, differentiated instruction, quality time, diagnosis and prescription, and teacher expectations. A teacher may have the best intentions, but if the proper materials are not used in the proper fashion, positive results will not follow.

Instructional materials are a potent part of the learning process. Moreover, the abundance of commercial materials for every subject area on the market today is astounding. The teacher can very easily become overwhelmed with their completeness and attach an unwarranted and naive emphasis to them. Quantity of instructional materials is not an issue, but has quality kept abreast with quantity? Unfortunately, such is not the case in many instances and one must be wary of using fancy-looking materials without first determining their quality. You have a great deal of control over this aspect of teaching. You should first make sure you understand the purpose of any intended instructional material. At times, materials are unduly criticized because they were not successful for a particular situation when in fact that was not the intended purpose of the materials. Second, make sure the materials are accurate. Don't assume accuracy—you are the expert. Many times instructional materials contain inaccurate information or make faulty assumptions regarding prerequisite knowledge students should possess to be successful with the new content. You must develop a self-monitoring, discriminating attitude toward instructional materials to ensure the quality of your instruction. Though materials are important in achieving instructional goals, you must always remember that materials are effective only in the hands of a capable teacher. Materials themselves are ineffective and can actually hinder student learning. However, the effective teacher uses materials in just the right way to "light the fire" and to achieve learning goals. In this sense, effective teachers always maintain a correct relationship to materials; that is, they utilize materials as their aids in realizing instructional goals. It is easy to become an assistant to

FIGURE 7.1 Software evaluation guide (at left) *(From* **Principles and Practices of Teaching Reading** *[6th ed., p. 530] by A. Heilman, T. Blair, & W. Rupley, 1986, Columbus, OH: Merrill. Copyright 1986 by Merrill Publishing. Reprinted by permission.)*

materials, and guarding against this pitfall is becoming more important today. Pressures are acute to follow a standard set of commercial materials blindly to ensure student mastery of basic skills, but this is not teaching. In this scenario the teacher is reduced to a mere technician. The effective teacher, however, selects and modifies materials to teach students what they need to know. Adjusting educational materials to fit the needs of students is sound educational practice.

Personalizing Your Teaching: Teacher-Made Materials

Effective teachers produce their own materials to help meet the specific needs of students. It is unrealistic to assume all students will profit equally from using the same textbooks or other commercial materials. The necessity for modifying existing materials and creating new materials comes as a result of

1. range and demands of your instructional purposes (developmental, recreational, corrective)
2. student variability (instructional level, preferred learning mode, learning rate, interests)
3. unique aspects of the community and current events (city, state, national, worldwide).

Designing and devising your own materials will meet these three major requirements. As a consequence, instructional time tends to be used wisely because students will likely be motivated to learn and interested in learning because you are personalizing instruction. As you know, teachers try their best to implement their diagnostic information and use appropriate materials and activities to meet student needs. You must be certain that the materials are accomplishing instructional goals. The better the match between materials and instructional goals, the better the chances for improved student learning. Your judgments are crucial in this area. Being creative and designing materials specific to your curriculum will allow students to be more successful. The number of ways to modify existing commercial materials and types of teacher-made materials is limited only by your imagination. Listed below are some examples:

comprehension exercises
vocabulary games
word identification and comprehension worksheets and games
language arts materials
math manipulatives
language experience books
learning centers
research projects

art and music additions to lessons
modification of existing textbooks
- advance organizers
- reader guides
- structured overviews
- taping of chapters
- changing the stated directions to fit students' needs and instructional goals

The key to producing materials is to realize that you know your students and program better than any commercial set of materials does. Work toward using a blend of commercial and teacher-made materials in the classroom.

Considerations in Using Materials

Good use of materials is the discriminating characteristic of effective teachers. How, then, do we delineate the specific factors to consider in using materials to best meet students' needs? First, you must know the materials assigned for use in your classroom and the range of materials that may be used. Knowing the materials means being thoroughly familiar with the material itself, its uses, and its contents. Without this first, "obvious" concern, the other considerations pale to insignificance. You can remain current with new materials in your field by reading professional journals and educational magazines. It is also helpful to ask other teachers and attend state and national conferences in your subject area.

Second, you should be concerned with matching the readability or difficulty level of the material to the competency level of your students. Even though it is difficult to achieve an ideal match at all times, it is important to try. For instance, it is extremely difficult to rely totally on a textbook whose difficulty level is at least three levels above the competency level of most of the students. However, your efforts to lessen reliance on a textbook, plus the students' motivation and interest in a particular topic, will affect how successful they will be in learning. Instead of relying exclusively on a textbook, you can draw on supplemental materials and utilize various strategies with the textbook such as the directed reading-thinking activity, reading guides, advanced organizers, and structured overviews to help more students succeed. In other words, what the teacher does can affect this "match." As a general rule, teachers should be aware of the problem of the match, attempt to use appropriate materials, and attempt to eliminate or lessen possible negative effects of using material that may be technically too difficult for students. One of the most popular and most effective methods to determine the readability level of printed material is the readability graph developed by Edward Fry (1977). Fry's formula plots the average number of syllables and average number of sentences per hundred words to yield an approximate readability or difficulty

Average number of syllables per 100 words

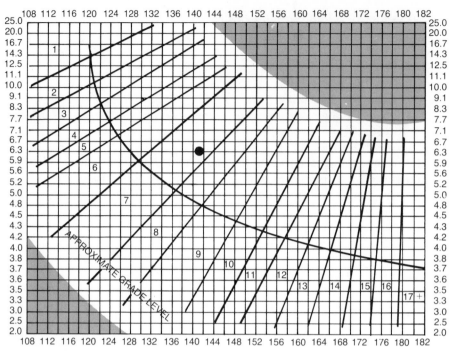

DIRECTIONS: Randomly select 3 one hundred word passages from a book or an article. Plot average number of syllables and average number of sentences per 100 words on graph to determine the grade level of the material. Choose more passages per book if great variability is observed and conclude that the book has uneven readability. Few books will fall in gray area but when they do grade level scores are invalid.

Count proper nouns, numerals and initializations as words. Count a syllable for each symbol. For example, "1945" is 1 word and 4 syllables and "IRA" is 1 word and 3 syllables.

EXAMPLE:

	SYLLABLES	SENTENCES
1st Hundred Words	124	6.6
2nd Hundred Words	141	5.5
3rd Hundred Words	158	6.8
AVERAGE	141	6.3

READABILITY 7th GRADE (see dot plotted on graph)

EXPANDED DIRECTIONS FOR WORKING READABILITY GRAPH

1. Randomly select three (3) sample passages and count out exactly 100 words beginning with the beginning of a sentence. Do count proper nouns, initializations, and numerals.
2. Count the number of sentences in the hundred words estimating length of the fraction of the last sentence to the nearest 1/10th.
3. Count the total number of syllables in the 100-word passage. If you don't have a hand counter available, an easy way is to simply put a mark above every syllable over one in each word, then when you get to the end of the passage, count the number of marks and add 100. Small calculators can also be used as counters by pushing numeral "1", then push the " + " sign for each word or syllable when counting.
4. Enter graph with average sentence length and average number of syllables; plot dot where the two lines intersect. Area where dot is plotted will give you the approximate grade level.
5. If a great deal of variability is found in syllable count or sentence count, putting more samples into the average is desirable.
6. A word is defined as a group of symbols with a space on either side; thus, "Joe," "IRA," "1945," and "&" are each one word.
7. A syllable is defined as a phonetic syllable. Generally, there are as many syllables as vowel sounds. For example, "stopped" is one syllable and "wanted" is two syllables. When counting syllables for numerals and initializations, count one syllable for each symbol. For example, "1945" is 4 syllables and "IRA" is 3 syllables, and "&" is 1 syllable.

level. Figure 7.2 presents the readability graph and directions for its use. The readability formula is also available in computer software (Fry Readability Program, Jamestown Publishers, Providence, RI, 1982). However, any method that assesses the difficulty level of printed material does not measure the influence of such factors as student interest, motivation, background of experiences, and the provision of differentiated instruction. Any of these factors naturally can help or hinder students' success in learning from a particular text.

Third, often the best uses of materials come about when teachers modify the original purpose of commercial materials to create a more meaningful and creative application. Students can often become actively involved in learning if materials are manipulated to fit their needs. This is precisely the reason that teacher-made materials are so effective. It is also a good idea to ask students how to modify instructional materials and to remember that the teacher's manual for a given set of materials does not know your students and your program. Keep notes on ways in which experienced teachers in your school have modified instructional materials.

Fourth, it is important to motivate students before using any type of materials. Very few materials are by themselves engaging or motivating. Time spent in preparing and motivating students to work with materials will pay off in student involvement and learning. The best materials are only as good as the teacher who is using them. In the hands of an exciting teacher, even dull materials can come alive and be effective in the classroom.

SELF-MONITORING FYI

Selecting and Evaluating Materials

With the multitude of materials available, it is mandatory you select materials that will help achieve instructional goals. The following guidelines are suggested criteria to consider when evaluating materials.

A variety of materials should be chosen to meet the different learning styles, interests, and kinds of reading experiences students need to have in your subject area.

The materials selected should be on varying difficulty or readability levels to meet the needs of students.

The materials should be consistent with instructional goals; that is, the content of the materials should match the goals of the program.

The materials selected should complement one another; that is, they should not be at odds with other materials in the program.

FIGURE 7.2 **Graph for estimating readability—extended (at left)** *Note: This "extended graph" does not outmode or render the earlier (1968) version inoperative or inaccurate; it is an extension. (By Edward Fry, Rutgers University Reading Center, New Brunswick, NJ 08903. Reprinted from* **The Journal of Reading,** *December 1977. Reproduction permitted. No copyright.)*

Practice materials should be selected in part for their procedural and motivational value when used without direct teacher involvement.

The materials should be consistent with a multi-ethnic approach; that is, do the materials avoid stereotyping and display a positive image for all ethnic groups?

The materials should present information in a clear and understandable fashion.

Students themselves should be consulted for their judgments and feelings when you select materials.

SELF-MONITORING FYI

Using a Teacher's Guide

In reality, you will most likely be required to use the textbook(s) along with a corresponding teacher guide or manual. Although the teacher guide was carefully designed, these manuals are often abused by teachers. Listed below are suggestions to help develop an appropriate relationship with teacher guides.

A teacher guide contains suggestions on how to organize and teach a particular body of content. Remember that the manual contains suggestions, not directives. Do not feel compelled to do or say exactly what is written in the manual. You—not the teacher's guide—know your students' needs. Use the best of the teacher guide's suggestions and your own modifications in teaching students.

Do not feel it is mandatory to complete each suggested activity from the teacher guide for your lessons. There are often innumerable suggested activities, and to try and complete each one is folly. Pick and choose only those activities (with your modifications) that students need.

Always look to supplement "textbook lessons" with other materials, especially teacher-made.

READER INTERACTION 11

Classroom Materials Inventory

Directions: Collect the materials that are used in the classroom in which you are working. For each material, decide if its purpose is developmental, that is, the primary text(s) of the subject; practice, that is, materials used for application or reinforcement; or recreational, that is, material used for fostering independent skills, abilities, and attitudes. After making this decision, write the name of the material under the appropriate heading. Next, for each material, cite the assumption(s) underlying its philosophy or use with students, and briefly cite its primary advantages.

CLASSROOM MATERIALS INVENTORY FORM

Purpose	*Assumptions Underlying Their Use*	*Advantages*

Developmental Materials

_____	_____	_____
_____	_____	_____
_____	_____	_____
_____	_____	_____

Practice Materials

_____	_____	_____
_____	_____	_____
_____	_____	_____
_____	_____	_____

Recreational Materials

_____	_____	_____
_____	_____	_____
_____	_____	_____
_____	_____	_____

SELF-MONITORING CRITIQUE

1. What is the motivational value of the main textbooks in your class?

2. Should students have input into the type of materials used for instruction?

Will your response differ depending on the subject area and instructional goal?

3. How can you modify existing materials to make sure students receive enough practice?

4. What is the relationship between academic learning time and appropriateness of materials?

Summary

Successful teachers select and modify a variety of materials to help maintain student engagement in learning. Materials do not teach by themselves but are vehicles to accomplish instructional goals. Whether materials are commercial or teacher-made, teachers carefully maintain a proper relationship to them. Considerations in using materials include thoroughly knowing the materials' content; knowing their readability or difficulty level and matching them to the competency level of students; creating different, more creative uses of existing materials; and motivating students to use any type of materials. The proliferation of computers in schools has highlighted the need for careful evaluation and selection of computer software. Quantity of materials is not a problem in the classroom today, but quality is. The effectiveness of the diagnostic prescriptive model is dependent upon selecting the proper materials to achieve goals and effectively using those materials in the teaching-learning situation.

References

Fry, E. B. (1977). Fry's readability graph: Clarification, validity, and extension to level 17. *Journal of Reading, 21,* 242–252.

Schaudt, B. (1987). Selected research in computer-assisted instruction in reading. In R. Zellner, J. Denton, M. Berger, & R. Kansky (Eds.), *Technology in education: Application and implications.* College Station, TX: Instructional Research Laboratory, College of Education, Texas A&M University.

Shalaway, L. (1980). Students' new classmates revolutionize education. *Educational R & D Report* (Washington, DC: Council for Educational Development and Research) 3, 7–10.

Principles of Instruction

- Cultivate student feelings and emotions.
- Maintain effective classroom control.
- Provide an appropriate balance between fostering direct learnings and inquiry abilities.
- Maximize the use of classroom time to teach students what they need to know.
- Diagnose student strengths and weaknesses and provide instruction based on student needs.
- Use a variety of materials to teach what the students need to know.
- **Believe in your ability as a teacher to make a difference and convince students that they will learn.**

CHAPTER 8

Teacher Expectations

Expectations for Students

Many of the qualities of effective teachers that have been identified in research on teaching have centered on the use of time, for both teachers and students, in the classroom. A second principle highlights the importance of what teachers believe. Research on effective schools and teachers has concluded that students learn more if their teachers hold high academic expectations for them (McDonald & Elias, 1976). For years, teacher expectations have been thought to be powerful indicators of student learning. It is a truism that your expectations for students in a learning situation may bias your actions and influence subsequent learning. In addition, students sense what is expected of them and behave accordingly. A teacher's expectations thus can become a self-fulfilling prophecy. Recent studies have reaffirmed the importance of teacher expectations and, more important, have provided details of how expectations are communicated into actions in the classroom.

Though it is important to hold high expectations for each of your students, it is perfectly acceptable to hold different expectations for various students. Your expectations should be realistic and reasonable, based on your diagnostic information. Having different expectations for different students is both natural and unavoidable. You hold different expectations for various things in life, for sports, entertainment, and the stock market, for example. If you did not have differing expectations for a learning disabled student in a math fundamentals class and an advanced student in an advanced calculus class, you and your students would have some uncomfortable moments in the classroom. Even though holding different expectations is normal, judgments and expectations must be based on up-to-date diagnostic information on school performance, not on sex, race, socioeconomic status, ethnic background, past school performance, or personal

129

characteristics. Also, your expectations must not be fixed in stone but capable of change based on student performance.

The possible negative effect on students of low expectations comes not from the expectation itself but how you manifest it in the classroom. Summaries of studies (Good & Brophy, 1987, pp. 128–129) have ascertained that these students

- receive less instruction and are expected to do less work
- receive less frequent praise
- are called on less often, receive less time to respond to questions, and are asked predominantly factual questions.
- are seated farther from their teachers, receive less eye contact, and are smiled at less often.
- are criticized more frequently for incorrect responses, and
- receive less help in difficult situations.

These students may receive inferior instruction all the way down the line—less allocated time, less concern for proper pacing of lessons, less content coverage in lessons, a lower frequency and quality of teacher-student interaction, and less support and encouragement from the teacher. A key word in the previous statement is "may." A teacher's expectations may not have negative effects on groups of students or individual students. Also, some students are not as susceptible to teachers' expectations as others.

Effective teachers believe their students can learn and communicate this expectation to them. It is important for you to be aware of your expectations and provide ways to ensure that all students are receiving instructional programs that meet their needs. To this end, teachers can focus on the following:

- Ensuring instruction is based on diagnostic information. The effective teacher is goal-directed.
- Providing sound instruction to all students. The effective teacher is concerned with providing adequate allocated time, time-on-task, balance of direct versus inquiry instructional goals, teacher-student interaction, lesson pacing, and checking on the academic progress of each student.
- Ensuring all students are involved in the learning process. The effective teacher checks to make sure all students participate in classroom discussions and other classroom interactions.
- Stating aloud to students your goals and expectations. The effective teacher continually verbalizes *why* they are doing what they are doing in the classroom.
- Enlisting parental support and communication. The effective teacher realizes the importance of involving parents.
- Making a personal commitment that all students will learn and exhibiting a caring attitude to all students. The effective teacher has a high sense of efficacy and is interested in each student as a person.

As future teachers, you should realize the powerful effects that your expectations can have on students. Though a number of conditions affect student learning, you have direct control over how you will interact and teach your students. The best safeguard against possible negative effects is to concentrate on providing the best and most challenging education for each student. This present recommendation matches what Arthur Gates, a noted authority in the field of reading, said fifty years ago when he investigated the necessary mental age required for success in beginning reading. At that time and for many years afterward, it was widely believed that students needed a mental age of 6.5 in order to be successful in learning to read. Gates's research disproved this popular belief and thus turned attention away from the child and toward the type and quality of instruction. He wrote:

> The most significant finding is the fact that the correlations between mental age and reading achievement were highest in the classes in which the best instruction was done and the lowest in those in which the poorest instruction was provided. More specifically, the magnitude of the correlation seems to vary directly with the effectiveness of the provision for individual differences in the classroom. (p. 507)

Teacher Efficacy

Effective teachers not only hold and communicate high expectations for their students but also have a strong sense of efficacy ("the individual's perceived expectancy of obtaining valued outcomes through personal effort"—Fuller et al., 1982). In effect, teachers with a high sense of efficacy possess a high degree of professional self-esteem and say, "I know I can teach these students!" Studies have shown a positive relationship between a teacher's sense of efficacy and student achievement (Berman et al., 1977, Ashton & Webb, 1986). Ashton and Webb's investigations led them to conclude that two separate dimensions comprise the domain of efficacy. First, there is a "sense of teaching efficacy," that is, "teachers' expectations that teaching can influence student learning"; second, there is a "sense of personal teaching efficacy," which "refers to individuals' assessment of their own teaching competence." Thus, teachers with a strong sense of efficacy believe teaching makes a difference in student learning, believe in their professional abilities, and believe that putting a high degree of effort into their work will result in higher student achievement.

Teachers with this high sense of efficacy know their subject matter well, like and respect their students, assume personal responsibility for the progress of their students, and believe in their ability to provide differentiated instruction to meet the varied needs of all their students. To become this high-efficacy teacher, one overriding requirement is a high degree of effort or commitment. Implementing differentiated instruction undoubtedly requires a great deal of effort, and teachers must have a high degree of commitment to the teaching profession. These teachers are motivated to put forth extra effort in teaching because they are motivated by pleasing results, not pleasing methods. Furthermore, high-efficacy teachers take the time and expend the effort to differentiate instruction in their classes not necessarily because they like to work in these areas, but because they are seeking satisfying results from their labors.

How do teachers maintain and increase their sense of efficacy? This is certainly a complicated issue, because efficacy is affected by a host of social, organizational, and personal factors. At this stage in your professional development, it is important to nurture those factors that are under your direct control. To this end, two areas require your attention: first, to continue to be a learner and to monitor and refine your professional skills; second, to realize that you are a member of a professional team and develop this collegiality in order to influence and change your profession.

In speaking to the issue of helping teachers believe that they can change things for the better in their classrooms, Goodlad (1974) stated: "They can do it if they can overcome two things—the feeling that they're not responsible for the quality of excellence in their schools, and the feeling that they're helpless to effect change" (p.4). The principles of instruction described in this book address themselves to Goodlad's statements and are based on the philosophy that teachers are responsible for excellence in their schools. The literature on teacher effectiveness has indicated the relationship between effort in selected areas and student achievement.

Professionals in every field work together. As a member of a profession, a teacher realizes he or she is a member of a team, acknowledges the expertise of other professionals, and seeks their advice or help when necessary. Teachers need to realize they will not be able to solve all problems by themselves and that they are not the only ones who may be experiencing a particular problem. You are encouraged to seek information actively from both your colleagues and various specialists (supervisors, principals, psychologists, social workers, speech teachers, reading teachers, and special education resource teachers) regarding an individual student's progress or lack of progress. Support and help are also available through professional organizations. They offer help in the form of educational journals, books, monographs, newsletters, and local, state, regional, and national conferences. Most important, these organizations provide vehicles for you to interact with other professionals experiencing similar concerns, successes, and failures.

Summary of Effective Practices

The study of teaching has made tremendous advancements in specifying how effective teachers teach. The primary purposes of this text were to present principles of instruction based on teacher effectiveness literature, to help you become more competent in the tasks teachers perform, and to help you develop a reflective, self-monitoring attitude toward teaching. The purpose of this last section is to highlight the necessity of maintaining such an attitude throughout your career. The principles of instruction will be brought together and presented as parts of a planned whole, not as separate entities. Although it is helpful to separate different teaching tasks for the sake of learning their distinctive features and applications, the effective teacher's performance is one of several principles that work simultaneously in his or her specific situation to achieve positive results.

Our growing understanding of the teaching process has also brought about a greater appreciation of its subtleties and complexities. Providing the right balance of instructional objectives, motivating students, presenting new material correctly to students, providing proper teacher-student interaction and feedback, and maintaining an adequate level of classroom control—these are but a few of the major areas demanding a teacher's time, expertise, and judgment. In addition, these teaching functions must be performed given the physical characteristics and limitations of the classroom environment and the wide range of individual differences found in each group of students.

Figure 8.1 summarizes some of the key areas relating to the importance of the teacher in the instructional program. With student learning the ultimate goal, the first area is knowledge of subject matter. You cannot teach unless you know the subject matter you are supposed to teach. Good teaching demands a thorough knowledge of the subject. Second, you should know your students, their developmental characteristics, motivational needs, interests, and academic strengths and weaknesses. Additionally, it is helpful to remember that student learning is affected by a host of factors ranging from emotional, physical, social, psychological, and neurological factors to out-of-school conditions. It is important to know this information about your students, but it is equally important to realize that your influence over these factors is minimal. Third, the principles of instruction serve as a foundation to guide your teaching decisions. They are attributes that need to be adapted to your particular teaching style, students, and the subject taught. Unlike the previous factors over which you have minimal influence, you have direct control over how you interact with and teach students. Fourth, without a professional attitude, knowledge, skills, and techniques will be ineffective. This attitude is first characterized by the admission that you cannot solve all problems in the classroom by yourself. A true professional realizes he or she is a member of a team within the school community and stays abreast of new knowledge and techniques by participating in professional organizations. Next, this professional attitude is characterized by a determination to reach every student, to base your instruction on goals, and to continually redesign the curriculum to fit the needs of students. Also, you must realize that the fact that no simple recipe is available for effective instruction in all situations with all students is exactly what makes teaching so exciting, challenging, and gratifying. Teachers need to continually diagnose their programs and monitor their instructional effectiveness. The principles of instruction presented in this book should be tried in your classrooms, and then tested, evaluated, and modified according to your situation.

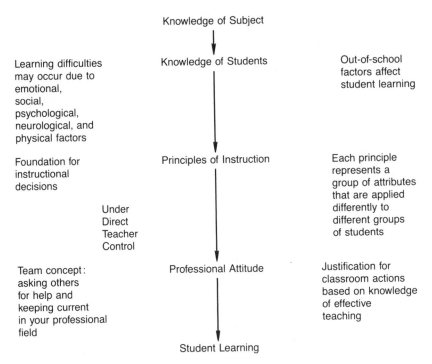

Knowledge of Subject

Learning difficulties
may occur due to
emotional,
social,
psychological,
neurological, and
physical factors

Knowledge of Students

Out-of-school
factors affect
student learning

Foundation for
instructional
decisions

Principles of Instruction

Each principle
represents a
group of attributes
that are applied
differently to
different groups
of students

Under
Direct
Teacher
Control

Team concept:
asking others
for help and
keeping current
in your professional
field

Professional Attitude

Justification for
classroom actions
based on knowledge
of effective
teaching

Student Learning

FIGURE 8.1 *Key areas in the teaching-learning process*

Most important, this professional attitude is characterized by justifying our educational decisions not solely on personal opinion but on principles derived from our knowledge of effective teaching. As a teacher you should be confident in knowing that what you do in the classroom will have a profound effect on students' lives. Go ahead and do what you think best in your situation but continue to learn and revise your thinking.

READER INTERACTION 12

Study of Classroom Interaction

Rationale: It may surprise you to discover that certain students are rarely involved in classroom happenings. The purpose of this assignment is to make you more aware of the interaction or communication patterns in your class. Ask one of your peers or your cooperating teacher to complete this form while observing you teach one or two lessons. Afterward, reflect on the information by answering the summary questions.

Directions: Using the seating chart, place a check (✔) in a student's block if a

SEATING CHART

question is directed at the student and a plus sign (+) if the student volunteers or initiates a positive response. Complete this assignment on one period during the day. If possible, complete for two days running for the same period.

Summary Questions
Which students were asked more questions?

Why?

Were there particular groups of students sitting together that received more attention?

Why?

Which students volunteered readily in class discussions?

Which students did not respond in class?

Why do you think they did not respond?

Teacher Effort Scale

In order to summarize for you the key points under each principle of instruction and reasonable information on teaching, Figure 8.2 presents a Teacher Effort Scale based on the principles of instruction. This scale does not claim to include all areas important in the teaching-learning process; rather, it indicates one way to view those areas in which you should expend time and effort in teaching based on both the teacher effectiveness literature and expert opinion. As previously stressed, the implementation of any principle is dependent upon teaching style, subject, and students. You are encouraged to rate your own efforts on each item by circling the appropriate number. In this way you can obtain a profile of your teaching performance indicating particular emphases. You may also ask a colleague or cooperating teacher to rate your efforts in one or all subscales. This will provide a snapshot of your teaching performance. You will become more conscious of your emphases, your strong points, and what areas to improve, modify, delete, or expand. By using the individual Reader Interaction assignments for the areas in which you desire improvement, you will be able to set new goals, reflect on your performance, seek out alternative techniques, and decide on any changes. Remember, you are responsible for the excellence in your classrooms.

	Student Affect						
	Rarely			Sometimes		Frequently	
Shows enthusiasm for learning.	1	2	3	4	5	6	7
Enjoys and respects students.	1	2	3	4	5	6	7

FIGURE 8.2 *Teacher effort scale*

	Rarely			Sometimes		Frequently	
Shows personal interest in students.	1	2	3	4	5	6	7
Designs learning experiences to enhance student self-perceptions.	1	2	3	4	5	6	7
Seeks to motivate students to learn using a variety of methods.	1	2	3	4	5	6	7
Shows sensitivity to the emotional needs of students.	1	2	3	4	5	6	7

Classroom Management and Organization

Clearly explains rules and procedures early in the year to students.	1	2	3	4	5	6	7
Prepares materials in advance and distributes them at appropriate times.	1	2	3	4	5	6	7
Plans for efficient transitions from one activity to another.	1	2	3	4	5	6	7
Selects and applies appropriate group management techniques to manage student misbehavior.	1	2	3	4	5	6	7
Monitors student progress by responding quickly and appropriately to student responses to material.	1	2	3	4	5	6	7
Delivers a lesson at an appropriate pace.	1	2	3	4	5	6	7
Attempts to involve all students in each lesson.	1	2	3	4	5	6	7

FIGURE 8.2—Continued

	Rarely			Sometimes		Frequently	
Differentiated Instruction							
Plans instructional lessons in advance.	1	2	3	4	5	6	7
Asks a balanced set of comprehension questions to tap both convergent and divergent thinking abilities.	1	2	3	4	5	6	7
Plans for a balance of direct and inquiry learnings in each subject area.	1	2	3	4	5	6	7

Plans and executes direct instruction for the learning of a specified skill or body of knowledge.
  readiness and overview
  motivation
  step-by-step explanation
  teacher-supervised practice
  feedback
  independent practice
  monitoring students' progress
  evaluation
	1	2	3	4	5	6	7

Plans and carries out inquiry instruction for the learning of high cognitive level objectives.
  readiness and overview
  motivation
  teacher explanation
  time provided for student exploration and discovery
  monitoring students' progress
  evaluation
	1	2	3	4	5	6	7

FIGURE 8.2—Continued

	Rarely			Sometimes		Frequently	
Waits for students to respond to questions.	1	2	3	4	5	6	7

Quality Time

Uses large and small group instruction to increase time-on-task and to teach what students need to know.	1	2	3	4	5	6	7
Uses all the allocated time for its intended purpose.	1	2	3	4	5	6	7
Shows evidence of time allocation for the developmental, recreational, and corrective programs.	1	2	3	4	5	6	7
Plans and monitors meaningful independent seatwork activities.	1	2	3	4	5	6	7
Shows evidence of time allocation for both direct and inquiry learning objectives.	1	2	3	4	5	6	7
Designs independent seatwork activities for direct learnings to be completed with a high success rate.	1	2	3	4	5	6	7

Diagnosis and Prescription

Utilizes results from informal and formal measures and observations to provide instruction suited to students' needs.	1	2	3	4	5	6	7

FIGURE 8.2—Continued

	Rarely			Sometimes		Frequently	
Keeps a record of students' strengths and weaknesses to pattern instruction to the needs of students.	1	2	3	4	5	6	7
Completes an analytical level of diagnosis knowing: achievement levels in class individual differences class needs which students are in need of further diagnosis	1	2	3	4	5	6	7

Variety of Materials

Seeks out and implements supplemental materials, textbooks, and games to teach the knowledge and skills needed for learning.	1	2	3	4	5	6	7
Produces teacher-made materials to assist in providing instruction for the specific needs of students.	1	2	3	4	5	6	7
Plans for a variety of materials to increase student participation.	1	2	3	4	5	6	7
Modifies suggestions in a teacher's guide to meet the needs of students.	1	2	3	4	5	6	7

Teacher Expectations

Involves all students in learning.	1	2	3	4	5	6	7

FIGURE 8.2—Continued

	Rarely			Sometimes		Frequently	
Bases instructional decisions on diagnostic data.	1	2	3	4	5	6	7
Interacts positively with all students.	1	2	3	4	5	6	7
Works cooperatively with parents and makes a special effort to contact parents concerning an individual student's progress.	1	2	3	4	5	6	7
Monitors one's own teaching.	1	2	3	4	5	6	7
Works cooperatively as a member of a team.	1	2	3	4	5	6	7
Shows a positive attitude toward teaching and continually strives to learn and to improve.	1	2	3	4	5	6	7
Thoroughly knows subject matter to be taught.	1	2	3	4	5	6	7
Assumes personal responsibility for the progress of students.	1	2	3	4	5	6	7
Seeks help if it is needed from fellow teachers and various specialists (reading teachers, special education teachers, psychologists, principals, guidance counselors, speech teachers, curriculum supervisors, social workers) regarding an individual student's progress or lack of progress.	1	2	3	4	5	6	7

FIGURE 8.2—Continued

References

Ashton, P. T., & Webb, R. B. (1986). *Making a difference: Teachers' sense of efficacy and student achievement.* White Plains, NY: Longman.

Berman, P., McLaughlin, M., Bass, G., Pauly, E., & Zellman, G. (1977). *Federal programs supporting educational change. Vol. 7: Factors affecting implementation and continuation.* Santa Monica, CA: The Rand Corporation. (ERIC Document Reproduction Service No. ED 140–432)

Fuller, B., Wood, K., Rapport, T., & Dornbusch, S. (1982). The organizational content of individual efficacy. *Review of Educational Research, 52,* 7–30.

Gates, A. I. (1937). The necessary mental age for beginning reading. *Elementary School Journal, 37,* 497–508.

Good, T. L., & Brophy, J. E. (1987). *Looking in classrooms* (4th ed., pp. 128–129). New York: Harper & Row.

Goodlad, J. (1974). *Report on preschool education.* Washington, DC: Capitol Publications, vol. 6, no. 2, p. 4.

McDonald, F., & Elias, P. (1976). *Beginning teacher evaluation study, Phase II, 1973–74.* Princeton, NJ: Educational Testing Service.

Sample Direct Instruction Lesson Plans

Lesson Plan—Kindergarten

Subject: Language Arts
Major Activity: Recognizing the *T* and *L* sounds at the beginnings of words

Instructional Goal: Given a series of pictures representing words beginning with the letters *T* and *L*, all students will be able to distinguish between the beginning sounds of the letters *T* and *L* with 90 percent accuracy.

Materials: Small barrel with pictures of items whose names start with *T* and *L* and a chart so that students can place pictures under the appropriate letter.

Motivation: Play the game "I Spy" in the classroom. The teacher spies a couple of things whose names start with the letters *T* and *L*.

Teaching: Explain that the names of the items that were spied started with the letters of the week, *T* and *L*. Have the students close their eyes and listen to the beginning sound of each word. Write the names of the items on the board and guide the students in using the words beginning with *T* and *L* in sentences out loud.

Supervised Practice: Have students close their eyes. They are to raise their hands if they hear you pronounce a word beginning with the sound of *T*.

Independent Practice: Play the picture game. Show small barrel with pictures of objects inside (beginning with *T* and *L*). Have each student draw a picture out of the barrel, say the name of the picture, and tell what letter the picture starts with. Have the students place the picture on the chart under the appropriate letter.

Evaluation: Observe and informally record how successful students are in distinguishing between the beginning sounds of the letters *T* and *L*.

Lesson plan reprinted with permission of Jill Renfroe Ruggiere.

145

Lesson Plan—Grade 4

Subject: Science

Major Activity: Learning the process of photosynthesis

Instructional Goal: After a brief lesson on how the plant's leaves manufacture food, each fourth grade science student will complete a checktest (in puzzle format) covering how roots, stems, and leaves serve the plant. The goal is 80 percent accuracy.

Materials: Bulletin board, to serve as a visual display.

The experiment must be started a week in advance. (For more details about experiment, see its description in the Plant Booklet.)

Experiment reaction sheet

Checktests for students to complete.

Motivation: Go over worksheets that students had completed the previous day. Review how water and minerals move through a plant. Introduce today's lesson: Yesterday we learned that leaves made food for the plant. Today we will discover exactly how the leaves make the plant's food.

Teaching: Using the bulletin board as a visual aid, show students how green plants make their food: A green plant takes water from the ground and a gas from the air. With the help of light, it makes sugar out of the water and gas. Then it adds things called minerals that it gets from the ground through its roots and makes other kinds of foods. This process is called *photosynthesis,* from light (photo) plus manufacture (synthesis).

Also explain that the green color in the leaves makes the food, with the help of light. The green coloring material in plants is called *chlorophyll.*

Supervised Practice: Pose the question: Can a green plant make food in the dark? Then check the experiment that the students had started the previous week. The experiment should show that without adequate exposure to sunlight, plants cannot produce the food which they require for growth. (See Plant Booklet for description of experiment.)

Independent Practice: Break students up into teams of four and have them answer the following questions on the process of photosynthesis on the experiment reaction sheet.

How are water and minerals moved in the plant?
What is the function of the leaves?
How do leaves make food for the plant?
What is the term for this process?
Can a green plant make food in the dark?
Why or why not?

Review with students both how roots, stems, and leaves serve the plant and how green leaves make food for a plant. Guide students to know that the roots of a plant absorb water and minerals from the soil. Water and minerals then go up through small tubes in the stem to the leaves. The leaves use this water and minerals along with the gas in the air (carbon dioxide) to make sugar. While making sugar, the green leaf must receive the energy from the sun. This food-making process is called photosynthesis.

Preview next day's lesson: Tomorrow we will examine the different places a plant can grow and how these plants are different from each other in terms of their roots and stems.

Evaluation: Each student must complete the checktest with a minimum of 80 percent accuracy.

Lesson plan reprinted with permission of Sally Sharp.

Lesson Plan—Grade 6

Subject: Language Arts

Major Activity: Letter writing

Instructional Goal: Following instruction, each student will write a friendly letter containing a heading, greeting, closing, and signature.

Materials: Sample letters, one per student (friendly, business, editorial, invitation)

Chalkboard

Language arts textbooks

Overhead projector

Transparency of letter to edit

Transparency marker

Worksheets (letter to edit)

Motivation: As students come into the classroom, hand each a sample letter. The letter will be either a friendly letter, a business letter, an editorial letter, or an invitation. After every student has read his or her letter, have the students see if they can label the different kinds of letters that are in the room. Write their answers on the board. (Prompt them only if necessary.) After the answers are recorded, ask the students if they can think of a situation when each type of letter might be utilized.

Teaching: Ask the students who have friendly letters to raise their hands and share the reasons for writing friendly letters. Explain in sequence the parts of a friendly letter. Put a sample friendly letter (that needs to be edited) on an overhead projector and edit it as a class. Review with students the parts of a friendly letter.

Supervised Practice: Pass out a worksheet containing a friendly letter that needs to be corrected and labeled. Complete the exercise with the students.

Independent Practice: Ask students to write a friendly letter.

Evaluation: Grading of friendly letter.

Lesson plan reprinted with permission of Myra Chickering.

Lesson Plan—Secondary

Subject: Science
Major Activity: Discerning similarities and differences between a shark and a perch.
Instructional Goal: Following an explanation and a confirmation lab, all students will be able to identify at least three similarities and three differences between a shark and a perch.
Materials (per group of four students): Dissecting pan (or large tray), one perch (or other bony fish), one shark (or other cartilaginous fish)

Soak specimens in water 30 minutes prior to use.

Precautions: Students may need to wear rubber gloves when handling preserved specimens. Relay any precautions indicated on the MSDS (Materials Safety Data Sheet) accompanying the preserved specimens.
Motivation: Review with students some of the characteristics of cartilaginous fishes. Inform students that today we will begin our study of sharks.
Teaching: Lecture/discussion giving students a summary chart using key words or phrases on the observable likenesses and differences between the shark and the perch. (If slides, transparencies, drawings, pictures, jokes, or cartoons are available, use them to illustrate the features and to elaborate on the functions, or theories about the functions, of the structures.) As the lecture/discussion progresses, question the students for their understanding. During the lecture/discussion, check each student's notes for completeness.
Supervised Practice: Have the students copy the chart in their notes. Remind them that other characteristics will be added to the chart as they continue their study of the shark. Ask them factual questions concerning information on the chart.
Independent Practice: Confirmation Lab: Use standard guided lab that shows drawings or descriptions of the structures.

To conclude, ask students: Would these characteristics be true for all other organisms in the same class (Osteichthyes or Chondricthyes)? Which one would be true? Remind students that there may also be differences and similarities internally and that they'll be studying them later.
Evaluation: Students will take a quiz assessing their knowledge of likenesses and differences between a shark and a perch.

Lesson plan reprinted with permission of Sandra S. West, Science Department Chair, Madison High School, Northeast Independent School District, San Antonio, Texas.

Lesson Plan—Secondary

Subject: Algebra I
Activity: Factoring Trinomial Expressions
Goal: Given 20 trinomial expressions of the form $x^2 + bx + c$, which can be

expressed in the product form $(x + d)(x + e)$, the student will determine the product form correctly for at least 18 of the 20 trinomials.

Motivation: Today we continue our study of polynomials by taking a closer look at trinomials. Specifically, we'll learn how to factor a trinomial—that is, how to express it as the product of two binomials. The ability to do this will be needed as we seek later to answer questions about the path of flying objects such as golf balls, a clown shot from a cannon, or an astronaut hopping around on the surface of some distant planet. We begin by reviewing what we already know about expanding the product of two binomials and about "removing" a monomial factor common to all terms of a trinomial expression.

Expand: a. $(x + 1)(x + 6)$
        b. $(y^2 - 3)^2$

Simplify
by Factoring: a. $2g^3 - 4g^2 - 8g$
           b. $4(x + y) - t(x + y)$

Teaching: Demonstrate the factoring procedure by using the example:

$$x^2 + 5x + 4$$

Note that this is a very special kind of trinomial—one for which the coefficient of the squared term is one. [The technique to be demonstrated will NOT work if that coefficient is a number other than one, but we'll see that it can be modified to handle such situations.]

We know how to "expand" products like $(x + 7)(x + 3)$ by using either the distributive property for multiplication over addition or the technique that is a consequence of it (i.e., the so-called FOIL Method). The result of that expansion is a trinomial. Now we seek to reverse the process by starting with a (special) trinomial and searching for the factors of the product from which it came. We say we *factor the trinomial.* The technique for doing this for every trinomial of the form $x^2 + bx + c$ simply examines b and c.

We ask:
- What pairs of numbers are factors of c?
- Which pairs of factors of c will have b as their sum *and* c as their product?

Consider the following example.

Factor: $x^2 + 5x + 4$
  a. Set up product form.
     $x^2 + 5x + 4$ $(x + \quad)(x + \quad)$
  b. Find *all* factors of 4.
     $(1,4), (^-1, ^-4), (2,2)$

    c. Find pairs having 5 as a sum *and* 4 as a product.
       (1,4) since $1 + 4 = 5$ and $1 \times 4 = 4$
    d. Write the product.
       $(x + 1)(x + 4)$

Exercises for Supervised Practice

1. $m^2 - 11m + 24$
   - Set up: $m^2 + {}^-11m + 24$ $(m + \quad)(m + \quad)$
   - Factors of 24: $(1,24), ({}^-1, {}^-24), (2,12), ({}^-2, {}^-12), (3,8), ({}^-3, {}^-8), (4,6),$
     $({}^-4, {}^-6), (2,12), ({}^-2, {}^-12), (1,24), ({}^-1, {}^-24)$
   - Pairs with sum of ${}^-11$ and product of 24: $({}^-3, {}^-8)$
   - Product: $(m + {}^-3)(m + {}^-8)$
2. $x^2 - 2x - 15$
   - Set up: $x^2 + {}^-2x + {}^-15 = (x + \quad)(x + \quad)$
   - Factors of ${}^-15$: $({}^-1,15), (1,{}^-15), (3,{}^-5), ({}^-3,5)$
   - Pairs with sum of ${}^-2$ and product of ${}^-15$: $(3,{}^-5)$
   - Product: $(x + 3)(x + {}^-5)$

3. $n^2 + 3r - 18$
4. $b^2 - 5b + 6$
5. $c^2 - 6c - 16$
6. $28 + x^2 - 14$
7. $20 - x + x^2$
8. $3s^2 - 6s - 24$
9. $35 - 2p - p^2$

Answer any questions and indicate to students that tomorrow we will factor another type of trinomial. (Work with individual students who need further explanation before independent practice.)
Independent Practice: Textbook problems on factoring 20 trinomials.
Evaluation: Student performance on independent assignment.

Lesson plan reprinted with permission of Kim Watson.

Sample Inquiry Learning Lesson Plans

Lesson Plan—Kindergarten

Subject: Math
Major Activity: Measurement
Instructional Goal: To understand the importance of measurement in cooking.
Materials: Large bowl, measuring utensils, flour, sugar, ginger, brown sugar, molasses, cinnamon, baking powder, shortening, and an egg.
Motivation and Presentation: Yesterday we learned to name one food and place it in the correct food group. Today, instead of working in small groups during math, we will all work together. We are going to talk about measurement and food (write the word "measurement" on the board and discuss its meaning with the children). Ask them the following questions: Have you ever helped bake cookies, a cake, or some brownies? Did you have to measure the ingredients in the recipe? Discuss how important measurement is when baking. Tell the children that today we will be making gingerbread men together. Read each step of the recipe to the class. Ask some children to help you add ingredients and others to measure. After completing the recipe, tell students that you will bake the cookies at home and then we will have them as a special treat on Friday. Conclude the lesson by asking the children why measurement is so important in cooking.
Evaluation: Student participation.

Lesson plan reprinted with permission of Kerry Scrutchfield.

Lesson Plan—Grade 2

Subject: Social Studies
Major Activity: Careers

151

Instructional Goal: Students will develop an awareness of the concept of a career, and the concepts of goods and services. They will hypothesize about what various careers would be like.

Materials: Film—"Why People Work," "Paper Connections" transparency, Career interview worksheet

Motivation: Have students project themselves into the future and imagine themselves as adults. What are they doing? Where do they live? How different will the world be?

Teaching and Discussion: Tell the students the definition of "career"—a job someone does to earn money so he or she can buy goods and services. Ask students for examples of careers. Ask students to imagine what various careers would be like. Which careers do they like best? Least? Why?

Discuss goods and services before viewing the film "Why People Work."

Make a job list on the board and separate into a "Goods" column and a "Services" column. Define jobs as those careers that make things for us to use and those that provide help in the community.

Use "Paper Connections" transparency to trace the careers associated with a particular product—a newspaper. Show a newspaper, and ask how much work goes into it. Proceed through the transparency as a group matching jobs (trucker, reporter, artist, lumberjack, newspaper carrier, editor, photographer, typesetter, proofreader, reader, paper mill worker) with illustrations.

Evaluation: Review what is meant by careers. Assign a take-home project for each student to complete. Students are to use the career interview sheet and interview an adult they know.

Lesson plan reprinted with permission of Beverly Boyce.

Lesson Plan—Grade 4

Subject: Science

Major Activity: Fourth grade science students will be taken on a guided fantasy and pretend to be a seed.

Instructional Goal: To grasp the significance of seeds by hypothesizing what it would be like to be one.

Materials: Handout for students entitled "Guided Fantasy" and worksheets for students to write about their experiences as seeds.

Motivation and Presentation: Yesterday we learned that many plants grow from seeds that flowers make. These seeds are often scattered by wind, water, and animals. Today we are going to pretend to be seeds. As I read to you about your experiences as a seed, I want you to close your eyes and try to imagine how it feels to be a seed. After the fantasy is over, I want you to answer some questions on a worksheet about your experiences. You can then draw a picture of the plant you finally became. Is everyone ready?

Guided Fantasy

Imagine yourself as a very tiny seed. You have fallen from a plant and are lying on the ground. You are there for several days without moving; nothing much happens. Then one morning a bird hops along and picks you up in its beak. He flies away carrying you far, far away. Then he drops you, and you fall down and land in a stream. The water is rushing very fast. You tumble about in the water, and float many miles downstream before you are washed up on the bank. You are so happy to be drying off in the rays of warm sunlight that you forget about the frightening experience you just had. Suddenly, you are picked up by some kind of animal, who takes you on a very long journey and drops you. You are very lonely because you realize that you are a long distance away from your mother plant.

Soon the wind begins to blow, and once again you are hurled through the air—up, up, and away you go, until you hit something very hard. It is a rock! You can't move now, and soon you feel dirty. Little by little you are covered by dirt until you are completely buried in the ground. The wind dies down and the air is very still and you are very calm. The evening comes and it begins to rain. It rains gently all night. In the morning the rain stops, and, to your surprise, you are growing roots. They are creeping slowly down into the ground making a permanent place to live.

After many days, you begin to grow a stem. Upward you get, peeking through the ground until you feel the sunshine on your face. Before long, you grow big, green leaves, and you keep on growing and growing. Now, look at yourself: You're a full-grown plant!

Discussion and Conclusion: Pass out worksheets for students to complete with the following questions:

What kind of bird picked you up? What color was he?

Were you ever afraid? Why?

What kind of animal carried you away? Was it big or small?

How did it feel when you began to grow?

Afterward, discuss some of the students' fantasies and help students to make the following generalizations: (1) many plants grow from seeds that flowers make, and (2) these seeds are often scattered by wind, water, and animals.

Evaluation: Collect completed worksheets and have students draw a picture of the plant they became. Design a bulletin board highlighting each student's work. All students participating in this activity will receive extra credit points for their creative efforts.

Lesson plan reprinted with permission of Sally Sharp.

Lesson Plan—Grade 6

Subject: Reading
Major Activity: Awareness of physical handicaps
Instructional Goal: Students will consider the possibility of being physically handicapped and possible ways to compensate for these conditions.
Materials: Story of a physically handicapped person; one dozen apples, oranges, or tennis balls.
Motivation and Presentation: The students will be asked to close their eyes. Once they are closed, instruct the students to untie and then retie their shoes. Next, have them get out a piece of paper and write their first, middle, and last names on it, again without opening their eyes. After completion of these two activities, have the students line up and, without using hands, pass an apple (or orange or tennis ball) from person to person. They should begin by putting the object under someone's chin, and then pass it from chin to chin. After the students have finished, have them return to their seats and then discuss how they felt when they were "handicapped." Discuss how they were or were not able to compensate.

Explain to the students that the story that they are about to read involves a boy who is forced to give up something very dear to him due to a serious illness.

Have the students consider the following purpose-setting questions:
- In what ways can Paul be considered a hero? (What traits?)
- What problem is Paul faced with?
- How does Paul deal with his problems?

Read the story "Return of a Ball Player"

Review the story by asking a variety of comprehension questions.
Evaluation: Ask students to write in their journals about one of the following topics:
- someone with some kind of handicap and how he or she deals with it
- an everyday kind of hero

Lesson plan reprinted with permission of Myra Chickering.

Lesson Plan—Secondary

Subject: Science
Major Activity: Discerning similarities and differences between a shark and a perch.
Instructional Goal: To observe and to compare bony fishes (Osteichthyes) and cartilaginous fishes (Chondricthyes).

Materials (per group of four students): dissecting pan (or large tray), perch (or other bony fish), shark (or other cartilaginous fish)

Soak specimens in water 30 minutes prior to use.

Precautions: Students may need to wear rubber gloves when handling preserved specimens. Relay any precautions indicated on the MSDS (Materials Safety Data Sheet) accompanying the preserved specimens.

Motivation and Presentation: Tell students that today we will begin a study of sharks and bony fishes by observing the likenesses and differences between a shark and a perch.

Inquiry Lab: Distribute one dissecting pan, one presoaked perch, and one presoaked shark per group of four students.

Have each group examine the specimens and discuss among themselves observable likenesses and differences between the perch and shark. Students need to be prepared to share these observations with the class.

Discussion and Conclusion: (a) Have one person from each group list on the blackboard their results and share with the class one likeness and one difference that have not been already listed. (b) When all the observable characteristics have been discussed, list all the features on a chart using key words or phrases as a summation. Students should make sure to copy this summary chart in their notes.

To conclude, ask students: Would these characteristics be true for all other organisms in the same class (Osteichthyes or Chondricthyes)? Which ones would be true? Remind them that there may also be differences and similarities internally and that they'll be studying them later.

Evaluation: As one person from each group tells about a characteristic, ask the class if they can also observe it (assuming it is correct). If someone cannot observe it, ask for a volunteer from the sharing group to go to the other student's table and point out the feature. (If slides, transparencies, drawings, pictures, jokes, or cartoons are available, use them to illustrate the features and to elaborate on the functions, or theories of the functions, of the structures.)

Lesson plan reprinted with permission of Sandra S. West, Science Department Chair, Madison High School, Northeast Independent School District, San Antonio, Texas.

This lesson plan is very similar to the "direct" plan on this topic. However, since this is an inquiry lesson, a specific objective is not given. Similar outcomes may be obtained, but less teacher control is exhibited.

Lesson Plan—Secondary

Subject: English
Major Activity: Studying Daniel Defoe and "The Education of Women"
Instructional Goal: Each student will demonstrate an understanding of the posi-

tion of women during the Age of Reason as presented in Defoe's "The Education of Women." Students will also understand Defoe's standpoint as a writer and his importance to his period.

Materials: Textbook, two handouts

Motivation: Give students a handout consisting of familiar quotations concerning women, primarily derogatory comments, in order to familiarize everyone (especially male students) with what women have had to put up with throughout the centuries. In order "to save his or her neck," the teacher will distribute another handout of quotations that praise and acclaim women and womanhood in general.

Teaching and Discussion: The teacher will receive a short introduction to Daniel Defoe and the students will read his essay, "The Education of Women." The teacher will lead a classroom discussion of the essay, noting both its positive and its negative aspects. Teacher will ask students for their perceptions of Daniel Defoe. Was he a crazed visionary, or was he just years ahead of his time? How did society receive him? What would the state of women be today had the changes that Defoe wanted to occur actually taken place?

Evaluation: Conclude the discussion by asking the students' opinion on the impact Defoe had on the time in which he lived.

Lesson plan reprinted with permission of Clay Gomez.

APPENDIX C

Additional Seating Chart Forms

SEATING CHART

SEATING CHART

SEATING CHART

Index

Academic learning time, 82–83, 93, 95
Activities, planning of, 33–35, 47
Affect learning, 13–14. *See also* Student affect
ALT. *See* Academic learning time
Ashton, P. T., 131, 143
Ausubel, D. P., 16, 28
Averch, H. A., 4, 10

Bass, G., 143
Beane, J. A., 13–14, *15–16*, 28
Beginning Teacher Evaluation Study, 81–82, 95
Benderson, A., 6, 10
Berger, M., 127
Berliner, D. C., 4, 10, 31, 48, 95, 112
Berman, P., 131, 143
Beyer, B. K., 6, 10
Blair, T. R., 3, 10, 102, 112, 119
Bloom, B. S., 66, 77
Blume, R. A., 19, 28
Brookover, W. B., 6, 10
Brophy, J., 4, 10, 21, 33, 37, *38–39*, 48, 130, 143
BTES. *See* Beginning Teacher Evaluation Study
Buros, O., 101, 112

Cahen, L. S., 95, 112
CAI. *See* Computer assisted instruction
Canter, L., 32

Canter, M., 32
CARI. *See* Content area reading inventory
Carlson, S. B., 102, 112
Cassel, P., 32
Clark, C. M., 59
Classroom constraints, 2–3
Classroom discussion, planning for, 66–68
Classroom instruction. *See also* Principles of instruction
  computer assisted instruction, 116–117, *118*, 119–120
  diagnostic decisions, 99
Classroom interaction, 134–137
Classroom management, 30–32, 88
  allocated time, 82
  effective control, 39–40, *41*, 42, 47
  problems and solutions, 45–46
  successful elements of, 33–37, *38*, 39
  teacher characteristics, 40, *41*
Classroom questions, constructing and monitoring of, 66–68, 74–76
Cloutier, E. F., 77
Cognitive learning, 13–14. *See also* Student affect
Combs, A. W., 17, 19, 28
Communication skills, 23–25
Comprehensive Test of Basic Skills, 100
Computer assisted instruction, 116–117, *118*, 127
Computer software, quality and quantity of, 117, *118*, 119–120

Computerized learning prescriptions, 116–117, *118*
Concepts of teaching, 6–8. *See also* Principles of instruction
Content area reading inventory, 101
Convergent thinking, 66–68
Cooper, J. M., 48
Cooperative grouping, 24–25
Copenhaver, R. W., 58
Corrective learning, 3–4
Corrective program, 3–4, 83, 95
Corrigan, D., 1, 10
Criterion-referenced tests, 99–102, 111
CTBS. *See* Comprehensive Test of Basic Skills

Dalgard, K. A., 77
Deductive method, 52, 55, 61
Denham, C., 81, 95, 112
Denton, J., 127
Developmental learning, 3–4
Developmental program, 3–4, 83, 95
DeVries, D., 25, 28
Diagnosis of instruction, 103
Diagnostic framework, 97
Diagnostic-prescriptive process, 96–98, 100, 106–111, 127
    computer assisted instruction, 116–118
    continuous diagnosis, 103–104
    expectations for students, 129–131
    informal measures, 101–102
    teacher observation, 102–103
    types of decisions, 99–101
    types of materials, 115–116
Diamond, N. A., 77
Differentiated Instruction. *See also* Teacher training
    definition of, 2–3
    individual lesson, 59–64
    learning, types of, 51–52, *53–54*, 55–56, *57–58*
    planning process, 58–59, 64–68
    teacher efficacy, 131–132
Direct instruction, 5–8, 62, 66–67, 79, 86. *See also* Direct learning; Lesson plans, sample direct
Direct learning, 5–6, 51, *57–58*, 78–79
    diagnostic information, 98–99
    functions of, 52, *53–54*, 55
    time emphasis, 82–86, 95
Discipline, prevention of, 32–33
Dishaw, M. M., 95, 112
Divergent thinking, 66–68

Dornbusch, S., 143
Dreikurs, R., 32

Educational diagnosis, 97–99
Educational objectives, 66–68
Elias, P., 129, 143
Emmer, E. T., 33, 48
Emotional maturity, 18–20, 28
Emotional security, guidelines of, 19–20
Engelhart, M. D., 79
Evaluation, 63–64, 71–74
Evertson, C., 33, 48
Evertson, C. M., 33, 48

Feedback, 24–25, 37, 62, 67, 88, 99, 133
Filby, N., 95, 112
Fisher, C., 81, 82, 95, 97, 112
Formal diagnostic measures, 99–100, 110–111, 117, *118*
Fry, E. B., 121, *122*, 123, 127
Fuller, F., 31, 48, 131, 143
Functional levels of understanding, 104
Furst, E. J., 79

Gambrell, L. B., 14, 28
Gates, A. I., 131, 143
Glasser, W., 32
Glickman, C., 32
Good, T. J., 4, 10, 21, 33, 48, 130, 143
Goodlad, J., 132, 143
Goodwin, S. S., 77
Gordon, T., 32
Green, T. F., 7, 10
Griffin, G. A., 31, 48
Group instruction, managing of, 33, 35–36, 48

Hansen, J., 48
Heilman, A. W., 102, 112, 119
Hill, W. H., 79
Hutchins, T. F., 4, 10

Independent activities, 86–88, 91–93, 95
Independent learning, 3–4
Independent practice, 62, 64
Independent program, 3–4, 83, 95
Indirect learning. *See* Inquiry learning
Individual lesson, 59–64

Inductive method, 52, 55, 61
Informal diagnostic measures, 99–102,
    107–111, 117, *118*
Inquiry learning, 78–79. *See also* Lesson
    plans, sample inquiry
    criteria for activities, 85–86
    definition of, 6–8
    diagnostic information, 98–99
    functions of, 51–52, 55–56, *57–58*
    independent practice, 87
    time emphasis, 83–84
Instructional control, differential
    emphasis, 87–88, 95
Instructional functions, monitoring of,
    70–71
Instructional goals, 2–4, 17, 36–38. *See
    also* Teacher training
    allocated time, 81–82
    computer assisted instruction, 117, *118*,
        119–120
    diagnostic decisions, 99
    direct learning, 51–52, *53–54*, 55, 82
    inquiry learning, 51–52, 55–56, *57–58*,
        95
    modification of, 97
    types of materials, 115–117, *118*,
        119–121, 126
Instructional materials, 60–61, 101, 133
    computer assisted instruction,
        116–117, *118*, 119–120
    evaluation of, 123–124
    major categories of, 115–116
    modification of, 121, 123, 126
    student motivation, 123–124, 127
    teacher-made, 115–116, 120–121
    types of, 115–116
    use of, 121, *122*, 123
Instructional outcomes, 87–88
Instructional planning, 58–64, 97, 111
Instructional program, 2–4, 17, 107, 133,
    134
Instructional strategies, 20, 28, 84. *See
    also* Teaching techniques
Interpersonal skills, 23–25
Iowa Test of Basic Skills, 100

Johnson, D., 25, 28
Johnson, R., 25, 28
Jonas, A., 79

Kansky, R., 127
Kierstead, J., 6, 10

Kounin, J. S., 33, 35, 48
Krathwohl, D. R., 79

Lasley, T. J., 31, 48
Learning outcomes, 87–88
Lesson components, 59–64
Lesson planning, 58–59, 64–70, 79
Lesson plans, sample direct, 145–150
Lesson plans, sample inquiry, 151–156
Lezotte, L. W., 6, 10
Lieberman, A., 81, 95, 112
Lipka, R. P., 13–14, *15–16*, 28
Logical activities, 7–8
Long-range unit, 65

Major activity, 60
Management, preventive strategies in,
    39–40
Management suggestions, 34–38
Marliave, R., 95, 112
Martorella, P. H., 48
Maslow, A. H., 17, 28
Materials inventory, 124, *125*, 126–127
McDonald, F. I., 6, 10, 40, 48, 129, 143
McIntyre, D. J., 58
McLaughlin, M., 143
Mental Measurement Yearbook, 101
Mini-unit, 65
Minimum competency tests, 100
Misbehavior, prevention of, *41*, 42, 48
Mohlman, G., 82, 95
Moore, J. E., 95
Morine-Dershimer, G., 48
Motivation in learning
    developing background, 61, 63
    student learning, *20*, 21–23, 28
    summary of, 132–133
    teacher feedback, 37, *38–39*, 63
Motivational strategies, 21–23

Newman, A. J., 19, 28
Norm-referenced tests, 105
Norris, W. R., 58

Objective-referenced Bank of Items and
    Tests, 100

Pacing, 42–43, 88
Pauly, E., 143

Planning, levels of, 58–59. *See also* Lesson planning
Praise, 37, *38–39*
Principles of instruction, 8–9, 132–134
classroom time, 80
diagnosis and instructional base, 96
direct learnings and inquiry abilities, 50
effective classroom control, 30
student feelings and emotions, 12
teacher ability, 128
teacher effort scale, *137–142*
variety of materials, 114
Professional attitude, 132–133
Professional team, 132–133

Quality time
academic learning, 82–83
dimensions of, 81–82
examining allocation, 83–86
independent activities, 86–87

Rapport, T., 143
Raths, J., 85, 95
Raths, L. E., 6, 7, 10, 18–19, 56, 79, 85
Readability level, 121, *122*, 123, 127
Record-keeping, 105
Recreational activities, 89. *See also* Independent program
Robinson, F. G., 16, 28
Rogers, C. R., 13, 29
Rosenshine, B., 5, 10, 31, 48, 52, *53–54*, 55, 83, 86, 95
Rothstein, A. M., 79
Rowe, M., 62
Rubin, L. J., 13, 29
Rupley, W. H., 102, 112, 119

Sadker, M., 48
Schaudt, B., 117, 127
Sedker, D., 48
Self-monitoring, 33
classroom management, 42–48
diagnosis and prescription, 104–105, 110
differential instruction, 68–70, 77
materials selection and evaluation, 123–127
student affect, 24–28
time management, 88–95

Self-perception, dimensions of, 14, *15–16*
Sequential Test of Educational Progress, 100
Shalaway, L., 116, 127
Sharp, G. W., 77
Shastak, R., 48
Shavelson, R., 58–59
Simon, V., 31, 48
Skill assessment programs, 100
Skinner, B. F., 32
Slavin, R., 25, 29
Soar, R. M., 87, 95
Soar, R. S., 87, 95
Sokolove, S., 48
SRA Achievement Series, 100
Stallings, J., 82, 95
Standardized achievement tests, 5, 110–117
diagnostic decisions, 99–101
differentiated instruction, 51, 66, 78–79
norm-referenced reporting, 105
Stanford Achievement Test, 100
STEP. *See* Sequential Test of Educational Progress
Stevens, R., 52, *53–54*, 55
Strategic activities, 7–8
Student affect
concern for, 13
emotional maturity, 18–20, 28
insights into, 25–28
interpersonal skills, 23–25
motivation, 20–23, 28
personal needs, 16–17, *18*, 19–20, 28
self-perceptions, 14, *15–16*, 20, 23, 28
Student needs, 16–17, *18*, 19–20, 28. *See also* Inquiry learning; Direct learning
diagnostic decisions, 99–104, 111
differentiated instruction, 51–58
instructional programs, 130–131
Student progress, monitoring of, 33, 36–37, *38–39*, 48
Subject areas, components in, 3–4, 83, 95
Subject matter, knowledge of, 133, *134*
Supervised practice, 62–63

Teacher effectiveness, 4. *See also* Teacher training; Principles of instruction
diagnostic-prescriptive process, 97, 130
direct and inquiry learning, 84–88
effective practices, 132–134

quality time, 81–82
teacher expectations, 129–132
use of materials, 120–121, *122*, 123
Teacher Effort Scale, *137–142*
Teacher expectations
  importance of, 129–131
  instructional programs, 130–131
  negative effect of, 130
  teacher efficacy, 131–132
Teacher-made materials, 115–116,
    120–121
Teacher observation, 102–103, 111
Teacher-prepared tests, 100–102,
    104–105, 111
Teacher-student interaction, 130–133, *134*
Teacher training. *See also* Principles of
    instruction
  basis of, 1
  computer assisted instruction, 116–118
  definition of, 6–8
  differenciated instruction, 2–3
  instructional goals, 2–4
Teaching. *See also* Principles of
    instruction
  basic element of, 59–64
  concepts of, 6–8
  definition of, 6–8
  effective practices, 132–134
  functions of, 7–8
  lesson components, 59–64
Teaching-learning cycle, 98–99, 111, 127
Teaching-learning process, *20*, 21–23, 28,
    134, 137. *See also* Direct learning;
    Indirect learning
Teaching tasks, 132–134
Teaching techniques
  classroom management, 31–33
  types of learnings, 51–52, *53–54*,
    55–56, 57–58
TenBrink, T., 48
Time, academic learning, 82–83
Time allocation, 81–86, 91. *See also*
    Quality time
Time, dimensions of, 81–82
Time-on-task, 87–90, 93–95, 99, 111
Turner, E., 3, 10

Unit plans, 64–65

Vacca, J. L., 101–112
Vacca, R. T., 101, 112

Wait-time, 61–63, 69–70
Wass, H. L., 19, 28
Wasserman, S., 79, 84, 95
Webb, R. B., 131, 143
Weber, W. A., 31, 48
Westbury, I., 2, 3, 10
Wilson, R. M., 14, 28
Wolfgang, C., 32
Wood, K., 143

Yinger, R. J., 58–59

Zahorik, J. A., 59
Zellman, G., 143
Zellner, R., 127